reality**check**
COLLEGE EDITION

the student's guide to the real world

grantbaldwin

Published by Priority Productions
Springfield, Missouri

Copyright © 2012 by Grant Baldwin

All rights reserved. No part of this book may be reproduced, stored in a retrieval system or transmitted in any form or by any means, electronic, mechanical, photocopying, recording or otherwise, without the prior written permission of the publisher.

Library of Congress Control Number: 2012932802

ISBN: 978-0-9818558-1-3

Published by Priority Productions, Missouri

Printed in the United States of America

Design and layout by Kelsey Davajon
kdavajon@gmail.com

First Edition

acknowledgements

Many thanks to:

My parents for instilling in me the values that much of this book is based upon.

Kelsey Davajon, for your wicked awesome design and editing skills. I owe you some Jimmy John's.

Kyle Scheele, for your wordsmith wisdom and writing knowledge. Your beard brings great joy to my life.

Lisa Klug (aka "The Rock Star") for helping manage my life and business. I love having you on our team! And Nicole and Rob are quite awesome as well.

My speaker friends for your input, knowledge, influence, and advice: Ryan Porter, Harriet Turk, Josh Shipp, Josh Sundquist, Jeff Yalden, Judson Laipply, Brooks Gibbs, Kelly Barnes, Rhett Laubach, Kent Julian, and Patrick Maurer.

Special thanks to Liz Kurt, Sarah Merrill, Kyle Holtman, and the Destination team at Iowa State University for your feedback on this project. You are truly some of the best people we work with and have converted me into a part-time Cyclone fan!

My three little girls, Sydnee, Emilee, and Mylee; you mean the world to me. There's no greater role that I have than being your Daddy. Thanks for your loving hugs and kisses when I have to "go talk to the kids" somewhere around the country :)

My amazing wife, Sheila, for your unending love and support. You're my best friend, and I can't imagine life without you. I wouldn't want to share this journey with anybody else. I love you, Pal.

table of contents

8   *Introduction*

COLLEGE LIFE

14   Will college be too difficult for me?
17   How am I going to pay for college?
20   Where do I find scholarships, grants, and free money for college?
25   What should I major in?
28   What classes should I take?
31   How can I develop better study skills?
35   How do I stay motivated with school work?
38   How do I avoid flunking my exams?
41   How do I become more involved on my campus?
45   Should I join a fraternity or sorority?

FRIENDS, FAMILY & RELATIONSHIPS

50   How do I maintain friendships/relationships when we're miles apart?
53   Is it normal to feel homesick?
55   Should I move back in with the fam?
57   My roommate and I aren't getting along… what should I do?
60   How do I deal with the social pressure to drink or do drugs?
63   How can I learn to embrace diversity?
66   How will I make new friends on campus?
69   Sex: If I love someone, why not?
72   This relationships is getting serious…what do I do?
75   When will I be ready for marriage?

FINANCES

80   As a college student, how can I earn money?
83   How do I make better decisions with my money?
87   Is it okay to splurge on myself?

table of contents

90	Do I still need a budget if I'm broke?
93	Do I need to get a credit card?
97	How do I build my credit score?
100	Do I really have to pay taxes?
103	Should I be saving money for retirement?
107	What do I need insurance for?
110	Should I be concerned about identity theft?

BEYOND COLLEGE

116	School, work, activities, life…how do I balance it all?
119	How do I create goals?
123	What do I want to do with my life?
127	Should I be networking?
130	How do I make my resume stand out?
134	What should I ask in a job interview?
139	Where can I find a great internship?
142	I'm interested in a unique career…how do I get started?
145	Should I start a business?
149	How do I find a place to live?

LIFE SKILLS

156	Who am I?
159	How do I learn to live on my own?
162	How do I better manage my time?
165	How do I deal with stress?
168	How can I learn to make better choices?
171	How do I develop better communication skills?
174	How do I deal with difficult people?
176	How do I get involved in community service?
179	What's my purpose in life?
182	How do I make the most of my life?

185	*Now What?*

introduction

You've waited for this moment your entire life. The moment when you can spread your wings, leave the nest, and try to fly. You've dreamed about growing up, living on your own, and being an adult in the real world. You're counting down the days until you will have the freedom to come and go as you please, to eat what you want when you want, and to listen to your music as loud as you'd like. You imagine having your own bathroom that you don't have to share with your disgusting siblings, not having to eat Mom's mystery meat anymore, and going to Walmart at 3am just because you can.

Maybe you're counting down the days until you leave your parent's 18-year prison sentence, or you've already been set free for the greener pastures of college life. You imagine how distraught your parents will be, weeping with emotion as you drive away from the house (only to later learn they had a party when you left). The air is filled with excitement, anxiety, enthusiasm, and anticipation as you grow up and prepare to enter college and the real world. But then it hits you like a ton of bricks…

A Reality Check.

The days of choosing between white milk and chocolate milk with your cookies are replaced by paying taxes, making career decisions, attending college classes, and finding an internship. Recess and nap time are distant memories that have now been exchanged for frustrations with your boss, relationship challenges, and the need for health insurance. Pretty exciting, huh?

Don't get me wrong. Growing up is just part of life, and this new chapter that you're entering into is one of the most exciting times that you'll ever experience. But if you're like most students, you have a mountain of unanswered questions about what to do next. When you think about it, life has been a pretty simple and steady routine up to this point. You've always been told where to go, what time to be there, when to sit, when to stand, and how to avoid making a fool of yourself in public. And while many of those concepts still apply to this new chapter of life, there is still so much that just seems unclear.

It's all incredibly thrilling, but it also feels incredibly overwhelming. You teeter between the feeling of "I can't wait to get there," and the emotion that says, "I miss my Mommy!" That feeling that you're experiencing is one felt by every other student who has been in your position. You're not the first one to feel that way, and you definitely won't be the last. You're experiencing something far too common…

A Reality Check.

So where do you begin to get the answers you're looking for about this transition to life in college and the real world? You probably have questions about choosing a major, moving away from friends, finding a place to live, making a budget, and living a balanced life. Plus the hundreds of other questions, cares, and concerns that race through your head.

Well, you've come to the right place, and hopefully I can help. Since we're going to be hanging out together for the next several pages, let me introduce myself. My name is Grant, and I've spent a good chunk of my life trying to motivate, inspire, encourage, and equip students just like you. Maybe I'm strange, but I actually really like students. While most adults find it easy to look down upon and criticize young people today, they may have forgotten that they were your age once. Clearly the old age and lack of memory is affecting them.

But we've all been in your shoes before with the deer-in-the-headlights look, trying to figure out what to do next. I know I've been there. But at the same time, I can think of numerous people in my life who helped me to make the transition into the person I am today. And I hope, in some small way, that this book is able to do that for you.

As you may have already noticed, this book is broken down into five main sections that address the common issues and questions that college students have about preparing for and entering into the real world. I cover issues related to college life, friendships and relationships, money, living beyond college, and several life skills. Also, I think it's important you know

I didn't just pull out a bunch of random questions for this book. I spent several months interviewing and talking with college freshmen just like you from around the country and asked them what questions they had about preparing for the real world. This book was formed based on their feedback and questions.

While you can certainly read this book in sequential order, you can also feel free to skip around and read about the most pressing questions in your life right now. There will be some questions that may not apply to you today but could come up in a few months or years. There are other questions that perhaps you've already answered in life, but you may need to refer back to in the future. This resource is *your* resource. My hope is that this book becomes a valuable tool to you, and that you are able to refer to it for direction and guidance on a regular basis. This is your book, so utilize it in whatever way makes the most sense for you.

Regardless of the order you read this book, I will ask you to do one thing up front. I'm going to ask you to commit to do something differently in your life as a result of what you read.

Part of the value of books and learning in general is that they allow us the opportunity to implement and apply new ideas to our lives. Far too often, something is just a "nice idea." We can see the value of applying it, but we never actually do anything with it. So as you read this book, I would challenge you to continue to ask yourself a simple two-word question: *Now what?* What are you going to do differently as a result of what you're reading?

Having said that, I will give you a little disclaimer about this book. I don't want to disappoint you, but this book contains no magic formula, secret pill, or special sauce for helping you to transition into the real world. Few things in life come with a simple solution, an easy explanation, or a quick fix answer. Life in the real world is a blast, but it certainly has its share of challenges. Although I may or may not have ever met you, I know that you can be successful. I know that you're smart enough to realize that success doesn't just happen. It's something that you have to work at on a continual basis.

I wrote this book because not only do I love working with students, but because I believe in students. I believe that you can live the dream you desire. I know I am. Is it easy? Of course not. Is it worth it? Absolutely. But it starts with…

A Reality Check.

section one

college life

chapter one
will college be too difficult for me?

While everyone is different, college won't be dramatically more difficult than high school for most people. In some ways it is more difficult than high school, in the same way that your senior year was probably more difficult than your junior year.

Is high school more difficult than kindergarten? Of course it is. But that's relatively speaking. Kindergarten should be easier for an 18 year old compared to a five year old. But kindergarten isn't designed for 18 year olds…at least not most of the time. The point is that each year of school is designed to offer a fair challenge for where you're at in life.

Each year of school may get progressively more challenging, but that's a good thing. You want experiences in life that will push and challenge you to be better. If you just stayed in kindergarten for your entire educational career, you'd never learn more than your shapes and colors (although you would be a whiz at tying your shoes and would utterly dominate kickball).

College isn't necessarily too difficult; it's just different. For the last 13 years of school, you've become used to the system. Go to school around 8am. Get out around 3pm. Monday through Friday. Wash. Rinse. Repeat. College is just a different experience from that. In college, you determine your own schedule. You pick when you'll take your classes. You decide when and where you'll eat lunch. You can even decide whether or not you'll go to class (although you should probably be there).

When you think about it, you're just learning a new system for school. Sure it will take you a few weeks (maybe even months) to get a good grasp of this new system, but you'll figure it out. Remember to give yourself some time to adapt. Don't expect to come in the first week of school and have it all down. This will most likely be one of the biggest adjustments in your life up to this point.

Your first few weeks you will probably feel overwhelmed. You'll question whether you bit off more than you can chew. You'll ponder the meaning of life. But hang in there…you'll settle into a rhythm. It may take some people longer than others, but you'll get there. If a few months in, you still find yourself treading water with your studies and are having trouble adjusting to college life, make sure to talk to someone. Whatever school you're at, I know there are support staff there to make sure you make a smooth transition. They want you to succeed. They want to help you. They're on your side. By talking with them or asking for help, it doesn't make you weak. It makes you wise. You'd be foolish to nearly drown and never ask for someone on the shore to throw you a rope!

Although some classes may be more challenging than what you're used to, the upside is you get to pick the majority of your classes. Sure, you've got your general education credits you have to take (math, history, science, etc.), but beyond those, you choose the subject matter. And generally, when you pick out the classes, you enjoy them more, even if it is a challenging class.

Overall, college is really your first taste of life on your own. Some people get out on their own and flourish, while others fall flat on their faces (figuratively speaking, but if you check out YouTube you can probably find some literal examples as well). The key is learning how to handle your own independence. As crazy as it may seem, you're an adult now. You can come and go as you please. You don't have your parents telling you where to go and when to be there. Your high school principal isn't calling you down to their office, because you were late to class too many times.

Many adults can point to their college experience as a pivotal time in life that helped shape and define who they are. You can really create life to be whatever you want from this point forward. In which case, college can either be incredibly difficult or simply challenging but still manageable. So what will your experience be? I'm not sure.

It's entirely up to you.

Part of the college experience is learning how to balance that independence. There's nothing wrong with having a great time in college, meeting new friends, and soaking up all the college experience has to offer. Of course there's the academic side of the equation that you came to college for as well. And really you can't go too far in either direction.

If you spend your entire college experience partying, staying up late, skipping classes, and slacking on your homework, then yes, I'm sure college will seem too difficult. But if you're diligent with your studies, keep up on assignments, study well for exams, you'll be just fine. But the decision is yours.

chapter two
how am I going to pay for college?

Although it's been said that "knowledge is power," they failed to mention that knowledge via a college degree would cost you an arm, a leg, and the naming rights to your first born. I'm sure by now, you've had the reality check that college can be crazy costly. In fact, according to InflationData.com, "The overall inflation rate since 1986 increased 100.14%, which is why we pay nearly double for everything we buy. During the same time, tuition increased 412.62%!"[1] Holy Schnikes Batman!

While we can all agree that stat is insane, simply throwing in the towel and resorting to a pile of student loan debt doesn't have to be your solution. Although you've got to get creative and bust your butt, you can pay for college AND still have a life. You're welcome. Here's how...

take community college classes

The average cost per credit hour at a public or private institution versus an area community college is a pretty big gap. Regardless of what you major in, there will be certain general education credits you have to take

---

[1] http://www.intellectualtakeout.org/library/chart-graph/college-tuition-fees-vs-overall-inflation

(i.e. math, history, writing, literature, etc.). So in order to save a few dollars, wouldn't it make sense to take a couple of those classes at a community college? This is exactly what I did. I took two semesters worth of general education classes at a community college, then transferred the credits back to the college I later graduated from. It saved me thousands of dollars. Be sure to check with the school you want to graduate from to make sure the community college classes you are planning on taking will transfer.

become a scholarship ninja

"Use scholarships to help pay for school? That's brilliant, Grant!" Thank you. I'm sure you're well aware of the potential dent you can make in your school bill through scholarships. Unfortunately, although most students know how beneficial scholarships can be, they don't bother with them. Sure, they're boring, tedious, repetitive, and dull, but they are worth the investment of your time. In fact, in the next chapter I'll show you how you can make as much as $50 per hour with scholarships. Intrigued? (Right now you should raise your eyebrow and stroke your chin in an intrigued manner.)

get a job

Although your school bill may be dramatically higher than the minimum wage you're earning, countless students continue to work to put themselves through school. Since you may just be starting college, you might be hesitant to want to get a job, so you can instead focus on your studies, get involved with a fraternity or sorority, and stalk that girl from your Chem 101 class. Here are two simple lessons that we'll talk more about in the coming chapters:

1. The older you get, the busier you become. That's life.
2. You've got to start making decisions based on the long-term and not just today.

If you bust your butt now working 20-30 hours while taking a full load of classes, are you going to be busy and tired? Yep. But if you graduate with no debt, it opens up an entirely new set of doors rather than being forced to take a job you don't want in order to pay off your school loans.

work-study programs

Worried about how a job might conflict with your class schedule? Lucky for you, there are some nice people on your campus who understand your situation. Unlike the manager at Applebee's. Confession: I worked at Applebee's in college. Many colleges offer some type of work-study program that allows you to have a part-time job on campus to help contribute towards the cost of your education. Check with the financial aid office to see what kind of work-study options may be available.

live at home

I'm sure after being out on your own, the idea of moving back in with Mom and Dad doesn't exactly strike a positive chord with you. But the cost of room and board is crazy expensive at most schools. I know it may be simpler and more practical to live on campus, but does the proximity justify the added expense? In most cases, the answer is nope. You'll be out on your own soon enough, but for now, consider heading back home to save some on the expense of room and board (assuming your parents haven't turned your room into their sauna). Personally, I lived on campus during my first year and then returned home. Despite a 30-minute commute to class, the savings from paying for room and board versus an extra tank of gas saved me thousands of dollars.

Sure college is expensive, and it's getting even more costly every year. But don't just throw your hands up in surrender to the high prices. Begin now to financially plan for college, so you don't get stuck paying for it for the rest of your life.

By the way, I created a free ebook called "How To Go To College For Free." If you're interested, send me an email at grant@grantbaldwin.com, and I'll hook you up with it.

chapter three
where do I find scholarships, grants, and free money for college?

The best kind of money is free money, am I right?! As you get ready to begin your college career and are creating your game plan to pay for it (you did just read the last chapter, right?), it just makes sense to find as much free money as possible. While getting scholarships and grants for college isn't extremely difficult, it does require a major investment on your part: time. You have to not only find the scholarships and grants that you are eligible for, but also take the time to apply for them.

I'm sure, since you're just starting school, that time is one commodity that is in short supply for you. I would assume that rather than searching for and filling out scholarship applications, you'd rather have a root canal. But remember, this investment of time has the potential to earn you some serious cash to help pay for school. It really is like an investment that can pay long-term returns. If you spend a few hours NOW finding scholarships, it could save you hours of work later trying to pay off student loans, which will also be accumulating interest at that point.

So rather than trying to convince you that scholarships are worth the pain and hassle, let's just do the math. Let's assume it takes you an average of one hour to fill out an application for a scholarship. Sure, some will take a few hours, and others may just take a few minutes. But most applications are fairly standard and consistent, so you'll be able to do a lot of copy and pasting with your answers and even some of your essays.

Let's also assume that the average scholarship you get is only $500. Not quite as exciting as a $20,000 scholarship, but hey, 500 bucks is still 500 bucks! Finally, let's assume you only get awarded 10% (1 out of 10) of the scholarships you apply for. Now with all that in mind, here's how the math breaks down…

APPLICATIONS	RECEIVED	MONEY AWARDED	$ EARNED PER HOUR
10	1	$500	$50
50	5	$2,500	$50
100	10	$5,000	$50
250	25	$12,500	$50
500	50	$25,000	$50
1,000	100	$50,000	$50

Obviously, in every case you're earning $50 per hour. Where can you get a part-time job making $50 an hour? Legally? Keep in mind too that we figured all of this on the low end. Let's say your average scholarship was $750 and you got awarded 15% of the scholarships you applied for…I like that math even better!

I know it's a lot of work, but let that math sink in. Let's go to an extreme and say you applied for 1,000 scholarships this summer and got $50,000. Most people don't earn $50,000 in an entire year! This could potentially pay for your entire four year education at some public schools! If you could pay for your entire college career with one summer of hard work, that would be killer.

Every year there are literally billions of dollars in grants and scholarships awarded to students just like yourself. That's not a typo….that's *billions* with a 'B!' And unfortunately, there are also billions of dollars in grants and scholarships that go unclaimed every year. Why? Because students didn't bother applying for them. So how can you take advantage of this and not miss out on the opportunity to earn some free money? Three simple steps…

find it

Think of it like you're mining for gold, or that you're a bargain hunter who has to browse through piles of junk to find the buried treasure you're looking for. While it may seem overwhelming, remember it's worth the time. In order to find scholarships, you have to understand what they are given out for. Scholarships are given out for a variety of reasons ranging from the major categories of academics, athletics, and interests, to other categories such as your parent's employer, community involvement, and ethnicity.

With all the technology today, the best place to find scholarships is online. There are a lot of scholarship searches online that are worth your time to look into. When looking online, remember this one principle: never, ever, ever pay for a scholarship search. I don't care if they offer you a new car; it's not worth it. There are a lot of scams out there that will make plenty of empty promises in order to get your money. Here is a list of free, reputable scholarship search sites:

- www.fastweb.com
- www.cappex.com
- www.scholarshipexperts.com
- www.scholarships.com
- www.findtuition.com
- www.collegeboard.com

In addition to online, check with your college for school-specific scholarships or grants they may offer. A lot of major corporations you've heard of and whose products you may use offer scholarships. Think about your hometown and the local businesses that may provide scholarships to college-bound students. There are several local civic groups and organizations (Rotary Clubs, Lion's Club, and Jaycees) that offer scholarships. Also check with professional organizations for the career you're pursuing, religious institutions, and even your parent's employer.

The bottom line is there's a ridiculous amount of money available as scholarships and grants. You may have to do some digging to find them, but it's worth your investment of time.

apply for it

Once you have found the scholarships you may qualify for, then you have to let the sponsors know you want that money! Here are some tips when applying:

every application is different
Some are just a simple one page form you have to fill out. Others require an essay, recommendation letters, and deed the title over to your car (just kidding…I hope). So just make sure you know exactly what you need to do to apply. I know you've heard it before, but read the instructions.

every dollar matters
It's easy to overlook the $250 and $500 scholarships because they don't seem worth your time. However, because many students think of it this way, you may have a better chance of getting those scholarships because fewer students will apply. Remember the math we did earlier? $50 per hour is looking real nice.

break it down into bites
The idea of filling out 1,000 scholarships seems overwhelming, so just break it down and set a goal for yourself. If you fill out 10 applications per day, you would have it done in 100 days or just over three months. Sure, you may not have much of a life during those few months, but remember the potential long-term gain for your short-term sacrifice. One student told me he spent two hours every weekend during his first semester of college searching for and filling out scholarship applications. As a result, he was awarded two scholarships totaling $1,500. Not bad for only two hours every weekend.

spend it wisely

Every scholarship is different, so make sure you know exactly what each one is for. Some scholarships are open-ended and may be spent on whatever educational expenses you have. Others are a little more specific and may only be used for certain expenses.

Make sure you find out if the scholarship is a one-time award or if it is renewable, which means you could receive that scholarship each year you are in college. If it is renewable, make sure you know what you need to do to keep getting the money. Do you need to maintain a certain GPA? What happens if you change your major? Do you have to stay involved with a particular group or organization?

Finding and applying for scholarships isn't rocket science (although you definitely need scholarships if you're studying rocket science), but it does require time and effort. If you don't get that scholarship now, you're going to have to either earn the money by working a minimum wage job or borrow it and pay it back at a crazy interest rate. Make the investment of time now to get the free money that's available.

chapter four
what should I major in?

This is usually a difficult question, because if you're like most students, your answer today may be different tomorrow. Many of us have this form of "job A.D.D." One day, one profession seems appealing, but the next day, something completely different catches our attention. There may be several different majors that sound interesting, so you may find it difficult to know which is the best choice for you. Most larger universities have over 100 majors to choose from. These range from the usual Pre-Med, Law, or Business Adminstration to the unique, like Professional Nanny (Sullivan University), Organic Agriculture (Washington State University), or Retail Floristry (Mississippi State University).

As you probably know by now, one of the primary reasons for choosing a major is to help create a more guided education path towards your future career choice. But of course, your first several semesters of college will probably be spent primarily on general education classes that are required, regardless of your major.

Because of this, there is nothing wrong with waiting a semester or two before you officially declare a major. Be sure to check with your advisor to find out the deadline for when you must make a decision. Also, you don't want to wait too long before declaring a major. Keep in mind, the longer you wait, the more likely you are to take classes that are not required for your major and could end up being wasted credits (and wasted money).

Even if you've known for your entire life what you wanted to do as a career, you still may give it a semester or two to make a decision. Have you ever had the experience where something looks really cool from the outside looking in, but once you actually have the experience for yourself, it's not what you signed up for? That may be the case with your career choice. You may have always wanted to be a scientist, an attorney, an accountant, or an engineer, but when you actually get up close, the career is not what you thought it would be. Until you nail down what you want to pursue, the best major is "undecided."

When choosing a major, one recommendation is to consider choosing a broader major as opposed to something extremely specific. That way you will have a wider scope of options in the future, should you ever decide to change career path, which you most likely will at some point.

Statistically, two out of three college students change their major at least once before graduation, and some may change it several times. According to the U.S. Department of Labor, the average college graduate will still change jobs once every three years and completely change career fields two or three times in his lifetime![1] While you shouldn't feel guilty about wanting to pull a one-eighty and go in a completely different direction, you also have to have a level of balance and focus. If you change majors every other semester, you'll most likely end up with lots of wasted credits, wasted money, and wasted effort. What happens to the squirrel in the middle of the road that can't make up it's mind which way to go? Bump bump. Road kill (FYI...I'm not suggesting you'll get hit by a car if you can't decide on a major.).

As you narrow it down and land on a degree choice, you have to ask yourself the question, *What will I do with this degree?* Remember that just because you graduate with a particular degree doesn't mean you have to stay on that career path for the rest of your life. I'm a perfect example of that. I graduated with a bachelor's degree and within a few years, I was already doing something different than what I went to school for. And there's a good chance in another few years I may do something different from what I'm doing today. However, there was still plenty of valuable information I

---

[1] http://www.thehilltoponline.com/news/college-students-change-career-paths-as-often-as-they-change-1.464504#.TxWLnmNWrK0

learned in college that I'm able to apply to my current career and business. The point is, just because you major in something doesn't mean you're locked into that career for the rest of your life.

Although for a while you may wrestle with figuring out what you want that major to be, at some point you need to make a decision, commit to it, and dive in. Depending on your college, they may allow you to remain "undecided" for only a few semesters before you are required to declare a major. Remember that because different majors require different sets of classes, the longer you wait, the longer you may be putting off taking classes you need in order to graduate. And that may lengthen your overall college experience, which makes it more expensive. With this same principle in mind, some of the classes you took for your previous major may not be necessary with your new major, and can become unneeded (and expensive) credits. If you're unsure about this, it is always a good idea to check with your advisor to make completely sure your existing credits will apply towards your new major.

Here's the bottom line: think through what you will major in but don't stress about it. While it is important, and you want to put some thought and effort into choosing your major (don't just throw darts at the list of majors). If you end up changing gears in the future, that's fine. It's not the end of the world. Find a major with classes that you love and go in that direction. Most students would rather sit in classes they feel they are really getting something out of and learning from, than go through four years worth of classes that they can't stand.

Realize that choosing a major is more than just choosing a particular career path. College is one of the first opportunities to truly prepare for the real world. You will not only learn from an educational standpoint, but you will also learn a lot about yourself. Deciding what you will major in is one of the first significant decisions you'll make now that you're out on your own. Take the time to think it through, evaluate your options, then trust your gut (unless you ate some Mexican food), and pick a major.

chapter five
what classes should I take?

In college, just like in most high school settings, you basically have two types of classes: general education and electives. By now, you know most of your first few semesters will be spent taking gen-ed classes that are required for your major. Often times, your major will determine which of these classes are required and at what levels. For example, if you are an accounting major, you will probably have several gen-ed math classes since you're going to be working closely with numbers. If you are a journalism major, you may not have as many math classes, but you may have several writing classes. To know for sure which gen-ed classes will be required for your major, just refer back to your course catalog or talk to your advisor.

Beyond gen-ed classes, you have electives. These are the classes that you are probably really looking forward to. It is in these classes where you begin to really dive in and learn about the specifics of your career path. Regardless of what you major in, most majors will give you some freedom and flexibility in the electives you take. And when faced with a course catalog with potentially hundreds of options to choose from, selecting classes that best serve your future becomes a little overwhelming. Here are some tips when selecting classes:

go wide before deep

The way most schools are set up, once you select a major, you then begin taking classes that really dig down deep into that subject matter. So if you major in accounting, before long you'll be taking classes like Tax Accounting, Accounting Concepts for Managers, or Accounting for Non-Profit Organizations. That's fine if you want to be an accountant for the rest of your life. The problem is you probably won't.

Our parents (and especially grandparents) were a part of a workforce culture that championed longevity and loyalty to a single company. While I'm a fan of both longevity and loyalty, I don't think those characteristics are as prominent as they were generations before. Why?

Our generation realizes that we don't have to be dependant on a company to take care of us for the rest of life. We realize that "job security" is a thing of the past. We realize that "job security" today means creating our own destiny. We realize that we like new challenges and opportunities, so the idea of sticking with the same job for the next 40+ years no longer sounds appealing.

So if there's a good chance you'll change careers at some point in your life (probably multiple times), does it do you more good to have taken really specific, niche classes or rather something more broad that allows you some latitude in your future career(s)?

Of course there will always be certain careers that require you take those deeper, more niche type classes. But for some of your other electives, try to select classes that will be useful beyond one specific career.

step outside your comfort zone

If you start flipping through a course catalog there will be plenty of classes that jump off the pages as having great appeal to your interests and abilities. Most of us would just prefer to take those classes if we could. We're naturally more drawn to things that resonate with our skills, passions, and talents.

But what if you stepped outside your comfort zone and took a few classes that on paper didn't seem like a natural fit for you? But why would you do that and waste credits on classes that you may hate? I'm not asking you to take classes that you know you'll hate. I'm asking you to try classes that will expand your horizons and help you explore subject matters that would not normally appeal to you.

When you think about the passions and talents you have today, I'm guessing they weren't all love at first sight. For a lot of us, the things we are best at and most drawn to were things we kind of stumbled across. Did you always know you had a knack for solving problems, giving advice, learning a new language, playing sports, or taking pictures or did you find your passion for that subject on accident?

How many other subjects, skills, or abilities are left undiscovered within people because we stick only to things we know and like? You never know. Maybe that random class you take will lead to a future career you would have never expected (i.e. Underwater Basket-Weaving 101 = huge job opportunities in the future).

think beyond today

Once you pick a major, you probably have a decent idea of what kind of career you'd like to do that aligns with the classes you'll be taking. But like we talked about earlier in this chapter, there's a good chance you'll have career opportunities in the future that go beyond the scope of your major.

So as you select classes to take, find classes that have broad appeal and value into the future. Think of your skill set like a toolbox. The more tools you have in that toolbox, the more "marketable" you become for potential employers in the future.

Once you land on a career decision, I'm a fan of really focusing in and drilling deep rather than being the "jack of all trades, master of none." However, when it comes to taking classes in college, I'm a bigger fan of the "jack of all trades" approach. This just gives you more options and opportunities in the future, rather than being forever pigeon-holed in a niche career.

chapter six
how can I develop better study skills?

I know you came to college to party, meet new friends, join a fraternity or sorority and feast on all the college life has to offer. But there's also that part about needing to go to class, study, and get an education. That's why you're here in the first place right? RIGHT? Sorry, I'm starting to sound like your mom.

Studying and keeping up on school work is different in college than it was in high school. In high school, you had Mom and Dad making sure you kept up on your homework as well as a teacher who didn't want you to fail. College is different. Mom and Dad aren't there to make sure you stay on top of your studies. And while your professors would prefer you be in class, pay attention and actually learn something, it's not their responsibility to hold your hand through the course. Remember, you're paying money (a lot of money) to take those classes, so in reality, whether or not you attend or study has little effect on your professor. Now of course most professors want to help you learn and push you to be successful, but your ability to pass or fail a class falls on you, not the professor.

In order to develop better study skills, here are a few tips to consider:

go to class

Again, this is different than in high school. Depending on the professor and the school, a lot of classes don't take attendance. If nobody knows whether you're there or not, it can be easy to assume it doesn't matter if you go to class. But it does matter. You can't possibly keep up with your school work and know what's going on in class if you're not there. If you need to skip a class here and there, that's fine, but don't make it a regular habit. Establish a routine of going to class unless it's absolutely necessary you be somewhere else (sleeping in doesn't count).

determine when (and where) you study best

Everybody is wired differently for when they're at their best. Some people do their best work in the morning before the sun gets up. Other people prefer the afternoon, while some are really able to focus at night when the vampires come out. Everyone is different. You have to determine for yourself when you are most focused, and then commit to that general time each day. For me, I'm generally at my best before noon. It's easier for me to focus and lock in on my work, whereas after lunch, I start to go downhill.

It's not only important to figure out *when* you're at your best, but also *where*. Studying in a loud dorm or frat house may not be your best option. The campus library, a local coffee shop, or a friend's apartment may be good options. If possible, carve out your own little space that helps you go into game mode. For example, I have a home office in the basement at our house, so I know when I go in there and sit at my desk, it's go time. That space brings a focus to my work, because that's a habit I've established. Working in my living room while my three little daughters are running around crazy just doesn't work. When and where is that place and space for you?

get a system for taking (and reviewing) notes

A mentor of mine used to always use the acronym "S.I.P." for *systems in place*. When you have a hot drink like coffee, you sip it, or else it burns you. This is true with taking notes in class. If you don't establish a good system for yourself from the beginning, you'll quickly find yourself drowning in a sea of knowledge. Although it depends on the professor, most classes will allow you to take notes on a laptop which many students have. Most people are faster at typing than writing, so this could be a good method for taking notes. Of course you may prefer to take notes by hand. Any option is fine as long as you pick one and stick with it.

One tool I would recommend for taking notes is a program called Evernote.[1] It's a free program that allows you to set up different notebooks, take notes, and then it syncs it all across multiple platforms. Meaning if you take notes on your laptop, it would sync those notes to your smart phone, your iPad or other tablet, as well as online. The search feature is top notch, so you can quickly find a specific note you're looking for. It also has the ability to easily share, so you could swap notes with a classmate.

One of the most effective methods for retaining information is to review your notes before learning new material. Part of your study time could include going over any notes you took from classes that day. It helps you to better process the notes you took and add additional thoughts that come to mind after class. Whatever your tool or system of choice may be, just establish it as a habit the first week of class.

join a study group

Many classes offer informal study groups that you can participate in. Study groups give you accountability to keep up with your classwork, but they also help you to better retain the knowledge you've learned. Most people retain more when they share or teach the concepts to others versus just writing down some notes. You may also gain some valuable insights from your classmates that you didn't pick up on.

Let's be honest: for a lot of students, it was fairly easy to get a decent GPA in high school. Most classes you could probably show up for, take a few notes (if any), pass some tests, wing a project, and score a B+ for the class. College is different. It's much more difficult and challenging. You have to not only realize that there's a difference in studying in college versus high school, but you have to change your habits to match the required effort. Just because you were a straight-A student in high school doesn't mean that college will be a cake walk for you. You may be in for a rude awakening

---

[1] http://evernote.com

if you don't establish some solid study habits in your first few weeks of the semester.

chapter seven
how do I stay motivated with school work?

Your first few weeks of college, it may be relatively easy to stay motivated and keep up on your school work. The syllabus is still fresh off the printer. The entire campus has that back-to-school energy and buzz. Even your slacker roommate is actually doing a little bit of homework here and there. That's generally the case for the first few weeks, but then the desire to do school work may start to head south for the winter.

It was the same way in high school wasn't it? Your freshmen year you were pumped to be in high school and wanted to give it your all, so you were staying on top of all your classwork and had some sense of motivation to do your best. But by the time your senior year rolled around, your battle with "senioritis" was in full-time attack mode. Because every member of our generation tends to have some mild form of A.D.D., we find it difficult to stay motivated and focused on a single subject over a long period of time. So how do you stay motivated with your school work? Here are a few ideas:

develop discipline

Discipline is a life skill that goes way beyond just school work. This won't be the only time in life that you're not motivated to do something you still need to do. Do you want to eat healthy all the time? Probably not. Do you want to exercise regularly for the rest of your life? I doubt it. But are those disciplines necessary to a quality life? Absolutely. So even when I don't feel like eating smaller portions or getting up early to exercise, I need that discipline that reminds me of the long-term value of what I'm doing. It's no different with school. When you have a better grasp of the long-term benefits of the classes you are taking and how they will lead towards graduation, it's easier to develop that discipline since you know what the end goal will be.

take interesting classes

It's easier to stay engaged in something you are personally passionate about. Now of course as we've established, not every class you'll be taking is a subject you'll be super stoked about. But as much as possible, take classes that you find engaging. What happens to time when you're doing something you love? It flies by. If you're really into something, you could spend 93 consecutive hours engrossed in that thing, and it wouldn't phase you. But if you're doing something you hate, it's as if time stands still. Not a good feeling.

keep a manageable schedule

Part of what makes schoolwork demotivating is when we have more on our plate than we can handle. If you're taking 18 credit hours, plus working a 40+ hour per week job, plus involved in a bunch of clubs and social groups, you're going to find yourself overly stressed and your studies will quickly slack off. At the beginning of the semester when you get the class syllabus, create a game plan. Most professors tell you up front exactly what needs to get done and when major projects are due. Instead of waiting until the night before to cram for a major exam or project, divide up the work over the semester. You'll be a lot more motivated to do one hour of homework per night rather than letting it all build up until the last minute.

Another key point to remember is that motivation is intrinsic. Even though I'm a motivational speaker, I realize that the only person who can motivate you is you (although that's not good for my job security). But it's true. Only you can motivate you. On an unrelated note, only you can prevent forest fires as well. Just a reminder.

A fair percentage of your life will be spent doing things you don't necessarily want to do. If you can begin to grasp now how to overcome those unmotivated moments in life, you'll be light years ahead of the game. As in Buzz Lightyears ahead.

chapter eight
how do I avoid flunking my exams?

Hopefully by now you realize college is going to be more difficult than high school. You're playing in a different league now. That just means you've got to learn to step up your game. Many students come into college intimidated by the potential workload. It's definitely going to be more than high school, but it isn't something you can't handle. Have confidence in yourself, establish some solid study skills and habits, and you'll be fine. Here are some tips and ideas you can apply to help you avoid flunking your exams:

pick the right classes for you

A big part of avoiding flunking exams is simply picking the right classes for you. Your advisor will be a big assistance when picking classes to help guide you to what you need to take. Try taking classes with subjects you feel comfortable with your first semester as you ease into the college experience. If you have several difficult classes that are required, spread them out as opposed to taking them all in the same semester. If you discover early on that a class is too difficult for you, talk with your advisor about dropping the class and taking something different. Before you drop a class, make sure you really ask yourself if you're just not ready for that class (but will be in another semester or two) or if you're just being lazy and don't want to take it. Dropping a class can definitely cost you some money, so make sure you know the ramifications up front before you pull the plug.

don't get behind in class

Getting behind in one or more classes can turn a snowball into an avalanche that is tough to control. When you slack off for a few days and don't keep up on a reading assignment or you miss some notes, you're immediately off course. In the next class, you'll be scrambling to learn the new information being covered while also trying to catch up on what you've been missing. It's like coming into a movie halfway through the film. You're trying to figure out what previous scenes you've missed while trying to keep track of the current storyline. It's much easier to just establish a plan and stick to it at the beginning of the semester.

utilitize support services

If you find yourself in a tough class where you're just barely treading water, don't wait to get help. Check with your school about tutoring or other student support services. Look into study groups from that class or find a classmate you can meet with to go over and review notes. Most professors keep office hours and encourage their students to stop by and ask any questions they may have. If you're drowning in a class, there's no shame in asking for help. If you wait until the week before the final exam to tell your professor, "I don't understand this class at all," you've probably waited too long and your professor is less likely to help you.

avoid cramming

Pulling an all-nighter and slamming a case of Red Bull is not smart or healthy. Although college students have a reputation of just cramming the night before a big exam, that strategy doesn't work. In order to avoid cramming as a last resort, you've got to stay organized. Know the various deadlines for your classes and keep a good schedule. Skip ahead to Chapter 43 about managing your time to see an example of how to plan out your school work for a semester.

We've all had that experience of walking into a class only to realize there's a test that day. Uh oh. Not a good feeling. It's a feeling of complete helplessness as you begin scrambling to review what few notes you brought with you. At that point though, it's too late. It's a much better feeling to walk into a class on a day you know there's an exam and feel confident, prepared, and ready. It's a good feeling when you're itching for the professor to pass out the exam so you can get started. You feel like "I got this" as opposed to feeling like "Oh dear God…I need a miracle right now!" Utilize the tips and ideas we talked about above, and you'll be fine.

chapter nine
how do I become more involved on my campus?

Regardless of the size of your college campus, there's a good chance it'll be easy to feel lost in a sea of students and the volume of opportunities to get connected on campus. How involved you become is really up to you, but your level of involvement will also play a huge part in your overall experience on campus. You may be that student that wants to get involved in anything and everything and truly experience all that the college life has to offer. Or you may be that student who wants to sit back and check things out a little bit before you dive into the buffet of options.

From the day you arrive on campus, you're going to be bombarded with amazing opportunities. Think about all the different ways to get involved at a college: Greek life (fraternities and sororities), student government, intramural sports, and of course, the endless number of student clubs, groups, and organizations.

Whether you're at a major state school with 30,000+ other students or a small private school with a few hundred people, I can promise you there's no shortage of potential friends and opportunities to fill your every waking moment. So how in the world do you even know where to begin? Let me give you a few points to consider:

go against the flow

Far too often students join something just because it is popular. If the "cool" people are a part of a particular club or organization, then whether or not we want to admit it, we assume if we're part of that same group, we will also be considered "cool." We do the same thing when making purchases. If I own a Mac or an iPhone or drive a Dodge Neon, my social status should improve (Wait, they don't make Dodge Neons anymore? Major disappointment.). This is what we call…STUPID! Regardless of who is part of a particular group or club, you need to find organizations and activities to be involved in that make sense for YOU.

try something new

College is a great opportunity for you to explore, investigate, and discover who you are, what you like to do, and what you're good at. And often times the answers to these questions can be found by trying new things. Think about some of the things that you currently like to do or are good at. Before you tried that activity for the first time, you probably had some preconceived ideas of what it would be like. However, once you got into it, you may have found it to be completely different than what you expected. And apparently you really liked it or it was something you were really good at since you still do it today! Try something completely random, but keep an open mind in the process…you may like it.

join groups that lead to something

I'm a big fan of the Stephen Covey philosophy, "Begin with the end in mind." This is especially true when it comes to joining clubs or groups. In middle school or high school, you may have joined organizations for the social benefit or purely because it was something fun to do. And while there should certainly be elements of that when you search for groups in college, you should also determine how participating in a certain group will benefit you long-term.

If you're an engineering major, being president of the hockey team probably does nothing for you. There's nothing wrong with being involved with the hockey team but taking on a significant leadership role may not be the best use of your time if it isn't leading to something. Keep in mind that the groups you join will provide significant networking opportunities with peers and possibly faculty or outside people who may open up future doors for you. So although there's nothing wrong with being a member of the clown club, chess team, and pep squad, make sure some of your involvement on campus connects to your future career and provides networking opportunities.

do something, but not everything

Most colleges and universities have literally hundreds and hundreds of options to choose from when it comes to what there is to be involved with. While it is great to have a lot of options, it becomes difficult to know where to begin. Think of it this way…

Have you ever been to a really huge dinner buffet? As in Golden Corral, Ryan's Steakhouse, and Old Country Buffet got together and had a love child (can I say that?). I've visited these fine, gourmet, five-star dining establishments before, and it's always a delight for my taste buds when I arrive (not so much for my stomach). These buffets have an endless supply of food available – all types and varieties. The problem with these buffets is there are so many options it's tough to know where to go. Do I start with a salad or go for the pizza? Should I grab some fruit or head straight for the ice cream? Do I eat chicken or fish? Peas or green beans? Ranch or blue cheese? There is no way to physically try everything that is available to you. There are so many options and choices that it can become overwhelming. You want to try everything but have no clue where to even begin.

The same idea applies to all the options you have at college. There are so many choices that it can become overwhelming. But if you go to a buffet and leave hungry, it's not the buffet's fault. If you overeat at the buffet and make yourself sick, that's also not the buffet's fault (but if you get food poisoning, you could probably blame that on the buffet). You can't try everything on a buffet, and you can't join everything on campus.

Pick out a few clubs, organizations, groups or activities that you are really interested in and start there. If you don't like them or a group isn't what you expected it to be, just get a new plate and go back to the buffet. While it's okay to spend some time with the "trial and error" method of finding groups to be a part of, you don't want this pattern to become your entire college career. Your first few weeks on campus will provide a great opportunity to learn and explore the entire buffet, so you can pick some groups that will really fit well with you.

chapter ten
should I join a fraternity or sorority?

By now, you've probably already established a preconceived idea of what joining a fraternity or sorority is like. You've seen the movies (namely *Animal House*) or heard the stories from older siblings or friends about some legendary Greek party. You figure if you can get into the right fraternity or sorority, your social status will be secured among the college elite, not to mention the endless supply of hot girls or guys that want to hang out with you.

And sure, being a part of a fraternity or sorority may give you a very small sliver of those things, but it's more than that. And as you've probably figured out by now, real life isn't always the way Hollywood presents it on the big screen. Joining a Greek community like a fraternity or sorority can offer some amazing benefits to your college experience. Here are just a few:

community

When you become a member of a fraternity or sorority, you're truly joining something bigger than yourself. It's more than just the existing members of that community, but you're a part of the bigger community of all members who have ever been a part of that organization. Have you ever noticed when Harley-Davidson bikers pass each other on the highway, they stick out their fist as an acknowledgement to the other biker? Why do they do this? Because they are acknowledging to one another that they are a part of the bigger Harley-Davidson community. The same thing is true with Greek Life.

When fraternities and sororities refer to members as "brothers" or "sisters," they're not messing around! You become a part of an extended family. That means when family members hurt, you share in that hurt. When family members succeed, you join in the celebration. When you join a Greek community, you inherit a support system that will be with you every step of the way through your college experience and beyond.

service

A major emphasis for most fraternities and sororities is community service. Whether it be through an investment of time, raising money for a cause, or simply helping out a fellow brother or sister, the idea of service is ingrained in the Greek culture. Most Greek chapters have a specific foundation or charity that they raise money for and help support.

academics

Greek chapters strive for academic excellence among their members. Most fraternities and sororities have strict GPA requirements. Chapters want the best of the best students to represent them. And I promise you that a GPA of 1.7 most likely isn't going to cut it!

networking

Because you are a part of that bigger community, there will be numerous networking opportunities available to you. Some fraternities and sororities have alumni services to help connect members with job opportunities. That shared bond of being a member of the same Greek community could open up potential jobs, business opportunities, and connections.

Depending on your school, Greek life may be a huge deal, or it may be a red-headed step child. If your college or university has fraternities and sororities, they also will have a Greek Affairs office. Stop by and ask questions to learn more about the options and opportunities available to you. Generally, you can also check out the school website to explore the various fraternities and sororities available for you to join.

Job security is a thing of the past. Today, job security means creating your own destiny.

section two

---

family, friends
& relationships

chapter eleven
how do I maintain friendships/ relationships when we're miles apart?

We all have those friends in life that we're so close to that we can finish their sentences, we know what they are thinking, and we could tell stories about them that might earn them prison time. Just a few hours in jail – nothing that bad! But anytime you move away from that person or any of your friends, the dynamics can tend to change. You may have moved away to go to college. Maybe you stayed in your hometown, but several of your closest friends went away for school. Perhaps as you are starting school, your friends are taking a completely different path in life. It's difficult to know how to handle or process such a transition when you've spent your teenage years bonding with this person or group of people.

It's not that you want things to change or that you plan on them changing, but often times they just naturally do. When you live in the same city, and see each other every day, there is a natural bond and connection that forms. But if you're 2,000 miles apart, that quality connection is difficult to maintain. It is certainly not impossible, but it is a challenge.

You've already figured out that as you get older, you learn more and more about who you are as a person. When that happens, it can naturally cause what you are looking for in a friend to evolve and change as well. As you look back over the years, you will probably notice that your friends in elementary school may be different than your friends in middle school. And your friends in middle school may be completely opposite from your friends in high school. It is not that one friend or group of friends was any better than any other group, but it is just the natural change that takes place. As you enter college and prepare for the real world, that progression will just continue.

Who you are as a person including your interests, passions, likes, and dislikes will continue to evolve and change. You'll find yourself more and more drawn to like-minded people. You'll probably spend more time with your new dorm or apartment roommates. You'll hang out with people who have the same major as you or who are involved in the same clubs, groups, fraternity or sorority. And naturally, you begin developing new friendships and may drift from existing relationships back home.

So how do you maintain those friendships? To start with, you really have to work at it. While nothing can replace quality time spent together, consistent and quality communication is a must. With the digital world that we live in, you can stay connected through email, blogs, Facebook, texting, and even video chat. When I travel to speak at events, I always try to video chat with my wife and daughters back home. Although I'm not physically there with them, it is amazing to be able to see them live. Ah, the power of technology! But if you talk on the phone or email back and forth only once a month, then how valuable can your friendship really be? So your communication must be both consistent and quality.

My younger brother is currently attending NYU in New York City. Because we only see each other twice a year or so when he comes to visit or I go out there, it requires more effort and energy to stay connected. Because we are not spending daily time together, we may feel more disconnected in those times that we do get together. Again, that's not a good thing or bad thing. It's just life. But he's still my brother, and so we make an effort to stay connected whether it be through a simple text message, a comment on Twitter or Facebook, or an occasional phone call.

As I think back to my friends from high school, there were some people that I was really close to that now I haven't spoken to in years. And others that I barely knew in high school are great friends of mine today. I say all of this not to discourage you that your friends will abandon you when you move away, but rather that you would realize that all friendships and relationships evolve and change, and that is okay.

chapter twelve
is it normal to feel homesick?

There is absolutely nothing wrong with missing your family or longing to be back home. You spent the first 18 years of your life with your family, so if you move out for college, it may be one of the first times you've been away from them for an extended period of time. Sure you went away to camp that one summer, and you cried yourself to sleep (you don't have to deny it…it's okay…I won't tell anyone), or all the nights you spent away at slumber parties. But to completely move away, when you may not see your family for several months, is a totally new challenge.

So when you're out on your own for the first time, it is completely normal to feel a little homesick. Well, except for your younger brother. Let's be honest. He was just a pain. But it's okay to miss everyone else. Whenever you live on your own for the first time, it really is that feeling of leaving the nest and flying away. You're becoming an adult now (it sounds weird to hear that doesn't it?).

You have to allow yourself time to adjust to this new situation. Especially if you moved out of state or somewhere really far away (like Never, Never Land or Narnia), there is going to be a transition time for both you and your family. The first few weeks you may talk on the phone every day, but as the year goes on, you may only talk once a week. It isn't that you are growing apart or that you love your family any less, it is just the natural transition that begins to take place. My dad and I have a great relationship (he was the Best Man in my wedding), and we live about 10 minutes apart, but I may only see him once or twice a month. We email and talk on the phone, but we may not see each other often. But that doesn't mean we're not close. It just means that we are both busy living life! The same thing may happen in your relationships. And that's okay.

When you move away, an interesting transition will take place in the relationship you have with your parents. Growing up, Mom and Dad are basically the bosses of the house. If they ask you to clean your room, it is usually not an optional request to complete only if it's convenient for you. But when you move out and are living on your own, your relationship with your parents will change. It isn't that you now have full rule and reign to disrespect them or never do anything they tell you. Think of it this way. As you grow into an adult, the role of a parent somewhat changes to that of a consultant. If I hire a consultant to help me with my business, their job is to provide feedback and advice, but it is my decision whether I will listen to that advice and apply it. Your Mom and Dad will be there to offer advice and counsel, but it is your responsibility to ask for it and determine if you will follow it.

If you've ever been in a serious dating relationship, then you know that the first few months are filled with goo-goo, ga-ga feelings and the belief that this other person can do no wrong. But the longer you're together, those feelings may begin to fade away and change. You still really like or love that person, but your relationship is evolving and maturing. The same will happen in your relationship with your family. Your relationships, not only with your parents, but with your siblings and your friends will change. Remember, it is not that you love each other any less, but rather it is just the natural evolution and progression of those relationships. And that's a good thing. You don't want to be Mommy's little doll baby angel for the rest of your life…or do you?!

chapter thirteen
should I move back in with the fam?

When you're a teenager, you are literally counting down the days until you can move out of the house, and be on your own. I'd be willing to bet you even experienced a few blow-up arguments with your parents when you "politely" reminded them of how soon you were going to be exiting the household. But now you're out on your own, and perhaps now you have the itch to move back home. That or it's a rash. You may need to see a doctor. That's a common feeling a lot of college students have (the itch to move back home, not the rash. Just clarifying).

Don't get me wrong. Living on your own is exciting. You have an entirely new set of freedoms you didn't experience while living at home, but it also comes with a whole new set of responsibilities. Because of that, you may begin to have some feelings of being homesick. Like I mentioned in the last chapter, missing your family is normal (except for your annoying little brother). There is nothing at all wrong with missing your family and even admitting that part of you would like to move back home. But determining whether you're just mildly homesick or if you should really move home can be a big decision.

If your parents are cool with it, and it makes sense based on where you live, I would highly recommend living at home for a few semesters while you're in college. You will save a ridiculous amount of money compared to paying for room and board at a dorm. The problem with living on campus is that it can be crazy expensive. When I was in college, I lived in the dorms for a year and then moved back home to save money. I enjoyed dorm life, and my roommate was and still is one of my best friends, but that doesn't change how pricey it is to live in the dorm.

Another factor to consider is how responsible and mature you are. Let's be honest…some students just aren't ready to live on their own. Some are irresponsible and would be a disaster by themselves! Although Mom and Dad don't need to hold your hand and change your diapers when you're 21 years old, sometimes just the added accountability of living at home is beneficial.

You need to remember, though, that if you are living at home, it doesn't matter how old you are, you are living under your parents' roof, and you need to play by their rules. If they give you a curfew, you need to be respectful enough to be home by that curfew regardless of how old you are. If they ask for your help with the laundry or mowing the grass, consider it part of your rent for getting to live there. If you're going to gripe about their rules all the time, then get a place of your own, and you may quickly realize how good you had it.

If you decide to move back home, understand there is nothing to be ashamed of, and there is certainly nothing wrong with living with your parents. You need to also remember that you can't live with Mommy and Daddy forever. As much as they love you, and as much as they may deny it, they are really looking forward to having the house back to themselves! I know it's comfortable and cozy in your bedroom with your Scooby Doo bed sheets and your Mickey Mouse night light, but at some point, you just have to grow up and move out on your own! Spread your wings and fly, young grasshopper. (Do grasshoppers have wings?)

chapter fourteen
my roommate and I aren't getting along…what should I do?

You're completely stoked about moving out of Mom and Dad's casa and into the freedom that dorm life has to offer. You can't wait to stay up all night hanging out and bonding with your new roommate over some Jimmy John's and Red Bull. You envision this perfect roommate that is the coolest possible dude/dudette in existence. Just being roommates with them makes your cool factor go up 10 notches. It all sounded great in your head…until you actually met your roommate.

You knew you were going to have problems when you walked in your dorm for the first time and there sat this topless, insanely hairy dude, trimming his toenails and wiping orange Dorito residue onto your bed. Awesome. Not exactly what you expected, huh? Especially if that dude was sitting in a girl's dorm…that would be creepy.

While colleges do work to try to match people up who would be somewhat compatible (although this is no eHarmony), there are bound to be issues when you have two random strangers moving in together. It's possible your roommate may be your new best friend, but it's just as possible they could become your new worst nightmare. Here are some things to remember when dealing with a difficult roommate:

is this a phase or is this the way it is?

Any time I'm in a difficult situation, I ask this question, "is this a phase or is this the way it is?" Generally, it's just a phase. If you and your roommate hate each other one week, you may be totally cool the next week. All relationships and friendships go through phases that go up and come down. Think about your relationships with those closest to you. Some days you love each other and other days, you want to punch them in the throat. That happens in relationships, especially with roommates. More than likely, if you find yourself in a rough patch with your roommate, it will pass just as quickly as it arrived.

have you addressed the issue?

Have you taken the time to step back and identify what the root cause is to your issues? It may be that they are messy, and you are a neat freak. It could be that you like the music loud, and they prefer you wear headphones. Perhaps you like having people over, and they are anti-social. It's easy to let issues spiral out of control and before long, you're mad at that person just because, but you have no idea why! You can't fix what you can't identify.

have you talked it through?

Once you've identified the cause of the issues, you need to be able to talk it through. You may be upset with them about something, and they had no idea that was even an issue. People aren't mind readers, so don't assume they know what you're thinking. If you have an issue, go to that person, instead of going behind their back to talk with everyone else about them. That's not cool.

can you ride out the storm?

If you and your roommate have been butting heads since Day 1, you need to talk with your RA, RDA, or some other dorm staff. A lot of times they can step in and help resolve a tense living situation. That's part of what they are there for, so utilize that resource. If you find that living with that roommate just isn't going to work, you can explore other options, but you may consider at least waiting until a semester break or the end of the year. You're tough enough to ride out the storm a little longer before you need to jump ship.

Dealing with difficult people will become a part of your life. How you learn to handle and cope with that is important. You'll have crappy bosses… horrible coworkers…pain in the butt neighbors. That's life. If you simply become the ostrich that sticks your head in the sand every time difficult people come around, you'll never get anywhere in life.

chapter fifteen
how do I deal with the social pressure to drink or do drugs?

No doubt you have probably already dealt with the peer pressure to do something you weren't comfortable with. We all know that social pressure starts long before students arrive at college. Perhaps you've already been offered the chance to drink, take drugs, or do something else you really didn't feel comfortable with. It's easy to minimize the pressure with the simple slogan of "just say no." And while that is solid advice, it's easier said than done.

It's sad but college has become somewhat synonymous with drinking. As a speaker, I often ask students in a workshop setting to give me characteristics that describe the stereotypical college student. Without fail, the words "drunk" and "hungover" almost always come up and incite a somewhat uncomfortable laugh from the audience – they know it's true. In order to stand up to this pressure, here are some tips to consider:

know that it may get worse before it gets better

While every college is different, it's generally true that once you arrive on campus, the social pressure to drink or do drugs only gets stronger compared to what it was in high school. In high school, everyone lived with Mom and Dad, so the opportunity to get into alcohol or drugs was severely limited. Sure it still happened but nothing like college. In college, Mommy and Daddy aren't there to make sure everyone is behaving. For some students, they feel like they've been under Mom and Dad's thumb for so long that they can't handle this new found freedom and go completely off the deep end. You probably know students who have done that or have heard of those stories. It's important to be honest with yourself about what college life is like. Peer pressure will always be a part of life, but there's a good chance you'll experience more of it in college than at any other time in your life.

decide now, not later

The time to decide whether or not you'll drink or do drugs or smoke or get involved in promiscuous sex isn't when you're being asked about it at the party. In that environment, it's much more difficult to say no. It may even be virtually impossible for you to say no. The social pressure of that moment is ridiculous. You have to decide before then what you'll do and how you'll handle those situations. By deciding ahead of time what your response will be, does it make responding with "no" an easy answer? Of course not! It's still difficult. But if you're trying to make a significant life decision in the heat of the moment, you're almost always going to make the wrong call.

don't put yourself in a bad position

I decided early on in high school that drinking and drugs weren't for me. Although they've never really had much of an appeal to me, I didn't want to get pressured into doing something I wasn't comfortable with. So that means I didn't go to many parties in high school. Sure I would have liked to, and I was certainly invited to most parties, but I didn't want to put myself in a bad position. Why put yourself in an environment where you know you'll experience a lot of peer pressure to do something you don't want to do? That's not my idea of a good time. That sounds more stressful than fun. I don't want to get bit by a snake, so I make a habit of not handling them. I don't want to fall off a cliff, so I don't stand too close to the edge. I don't want to get burned, so I don't see how close I can get to the fire before I feel the heat.

the power of numbers

Standing up to peer pressure when you're on your own is extremely difficult. Nobody wants to feel like they're on an island. It's much easier to stand up for what you believe in when you know your friends have got your back. It's easier to go to a party and turn down the opportunity to drink if you know your best friend is standing next to you not holding a beer. When you have friends that share the same belief that you do about drinking or drugs, it's easier to be with those people, because you know they're not going to be pressuring you.

Unfortunately, college isn't the last time you'll deal with peer pressure. In life, you'll be pressured to cut corners with your integrity, cheat a little bit on that expense report or your taxes, tell a little white lie that won't hurt anyone. The social situations you find yourself in may change, but the pressure is always going to be there. If you start giving in to that pressure now, why do you think it would be any different when you're in your 30s or 40s? Make a commitment and covenant with yourself today for how you're going to deal with these situations and then hold your ground.

chapter sixteen
how can I learn to embrace diversity?

College can often times be like a melting pot of ethnicities, religions, colors, and backgrounds. Regardless of the size of your school, there's a good chance you'll experience a bit of culture shock when you arrive on campus. That's probably a good thing!

For the last 18 years, all you have known has been your little bubble of the world. There's a good chance you have grown up with the same people in the same town going to the same school for most of your life up until this point. You may even arrive on campus and quickly wonder if you've stepped into another world! A lot of bigger schools have students from every state on campus as well as up to 100 different countries represented! It can be a huge eye-opening experience to arrive to something like this if it's not what you're used to.

Most of us were raised a particular way with a particular belief system. And generally that's a pretty good thing. We all probably prefer that our parents raise us with at least some type of belief system as opposed to nothing at all. As a parent of three young daughters, my wife and I are raising them from our particular worldview and belief system. Most of us not only grew up with that worldview that's been given to us, but most of our peers and family members share the same beliefs. So perhaps it's been fairly rare to encounter someone who looked different, acted different, or believed something significantly different than you.

And then you arrive at college. And it all changes.

Realistically, college is probably a better representation of how the world really is versus how we were raised. I don't say that to take anything away from our parents or how we were raised. College is just a blend of a lot of different cultures and beliefs as is the case in the real world of life. And when you get to college, it can be a bit overwhelming at first. So how do you adjust to this new culture and learn to embrace diversity? Here are some thoughts:

realize the world is bigger than you

Earth is a seriously big planet. Bigger than you or I can even begin to comprehend. There's nothing wrong with your worldview or how you were raised, but there are a lot of other people on this planet besides you. So of course not everyone is going to agree or see eye to eye. You might meet someone who is a different religion than you. Or has a different sexual orientation than you. Or has a different color skin than you. Or voted different than you. Or comes from a different state or country than you. Or who doesn't look, sound, or act like you. And that's okay.

acknowledge and appreciate differences

You don't have to pretend like diversity doesn't exist. There's no need to lock yourself in a room, so you don't have to interact with someone who is different than you. It's okay to acknowledge and appreciate the differences among us all. Can you imagine how boring and dull the world would be if everyone was like you? (That's not to imply that you are boring or dull!) We need our differences to mix things up. Often times when you hear out someone who sees the world differently than you, your own worldview expands a little.

choose respect over bring right

The challenge for a lot of us, when it comes to accepting and embracing diversity, is our need to be right. The problem with our need to be right is that by default, it makes the other person wrong. Embracing diversity is not about deciding who's right and who's wrong, but recognizing that we can each be different, and choosing to be okay with that. I may not agree with everything you do, say, or believe, but I will respect you as a fellow human being. You deserve that right as much as I do.

Arriving on campus to a mix of cultures and backgrounds may be a slightly intimidating experience for you. But it doesn't have to be. Learn to acknowledge, appreciate, and accept diversity while you're in college. It'll make the rest of your life (and the lives of those around you) much easier if you do.

chapter seventeen
how will I make new friends on campus?

The first time you move away from home is one of the most exhilarating and exciting feelings. However, as reality settles in, it can be one of the loneliest and scariest feelings. When you live in your hometown under a roof with your parents, it can become easy to take for granted how good you really have it. You probably have friends that live in your neighborhood and buddies that you've known since kindergarten. (Don't you miss the nap times in kindergarten? That was random.) But once you move away to college, you may feel like all of that has been left behind. And in a sense, that is true.

The reality is that after high school, when friends begin to move away for college or job opportunities, you will naturally drift apart from some friends, and there will be others you will stay very connected with. You may have already noticed this taking place. It is not that you mean to lose touch with someone or that you're mad at them, it's just that life has taken you in different directions. There is always some level of turnover with your friends. You will always be in a place in life where you will be making new friends. It isn't something that happens just when you graduate high school or move away. It is part of growing up and maturing in life. With that in mind, here are a few of things to consider when it comes to making friends:

friendships take time to develop

They don't happen overnight, so don't expect a "microwave" process. Think about your current friendships. None of them just happened. They take time. You have your ups and downs and highs and lows, but those are the moments that solidify and strengthen your friendship. There is the old saying that "Rome wasn't built in a day." The same is true for friendships. For anything to have any lasting significance, it needs time to grow and develop.

making friends is risky business

Any time you try to start a friendship or relationship with another person, you are taking a risk. You are taking the chance that the other person may not like you, they may stab you in the back sometime in the future, or maybe they think you smell (do you?). You have to be willing to fully put yourself out there in a vulnerable position, although you may not get the same positive response back.

friendships don't just happen

You have to be proactive when it comes to making friends. I hate to burst your bubble, but when you move to a new area where you don't know anyone, people won't be lining up at your door to be your friend. It is not always like you see in the movies where people bring you baked cookies the day you move in! So if people aren't banging down your door to be your friend, that means the ball is in your court to go out and find them.

meet people where you live life

Odds are you're not going to find friends by browsing the personals, posting a message online or asking people at Walmart to be your friend. You're more likely to find new friends in the places you already live life. In college, you'll likely click well with people who are studying the same major as you. You can also meet people at the places you hang out (not Walmart), where you work, and even getting to know people in your dorm or apartment complex.

you won't meet people sitting in your room

Meeting new people and making new friendships is generally intimidating for most people. It's such a big risk to put yourself out there, that most people will resort to not even trying. Especially given the technology that we have and the social networks that are available, it would be easy to become a hermit and only interact with people in an online setting. But you'll never meet anyone sitting in your room. During your first few weeks on campus, your college or university will most likely have several different mixers and ice breakers going on. Don't miss out on those opportunities. Some of your best friends in college will be the people you meet the first few weeks of classes. In addition to the social mixers your school may offer, check out the various clubs, groups, organizations, Greek community, intramurals, etc. There are an insane number of opportunities to meet new people on your campus.

Even after I list all these possibilities for you, there are still some friendships that just happen completely randomly. One of your best friends is probably someone you disliked at one point, and another friend is someone who is a complete opposite from you. So when it comes to making new friendships, use the famous Nike slogan – get out there and "Just Do It!"

chapter eighteen
sex: if I love someone, why not?

Ok, let's be honest for a second. You started flipping through the table of contents just a second ago, saw those three big letters staring back at you, and you immediately came to this chapter! Maybe this should be the introduction chapter, since all students want to read about this first anyway! So since you're here, let's go ahead and talk about that big, scary word…SEX.

Often times, students think, "If I love someone, why shouldn't we have sex? It is our way to express our love for one another." (Either that, or you are both in heat.) But the truth is that having premarital sex can cause much more long-term pain than it's worth. I understand there is a lot of pressure to have sex, and sometimes it is just the sheer curiosity to know what it is like. But whenever you're involved with premarital sex, you're trading a moment of pleasure for a potential lifetime of pain. To me, it's not worth the risk. Here are some risks with premarital sex:

diseases

Let me just cut to the chase with the facts: Researchers at Stanford University found at least one in four college students has a sexually transmitted disease. In the larger population, this works out to 50% of people getting an STD at some point in their life. The Center for Disease Control estimates that 19 million new sexually transmitted infections occur each year, almost half among 15 to 24 year olds.[1] In fact, 80% of people who have a sexually transmitted disease experience no noticeable symptoms.[2] This usually means since nothing appears to be wrong, you're less likely to visit a doctor and more likely to spread a disease to others. Keep in mind that just because you can't see the effects of an STD doesn't mean it's not there. I understand that you're out on your own now, so you may go overboard as you adjust to your new found freedom. But if there's a time to be responsible, it's got to be with your health.

pregnancy

Chances are you knew of a girl in high school or in your community who was pregnant or had a baby while in school. As I travel around the country speaking, I'm amazed at the number of young women I meet who are pregnant. According to one study, 24% of college women will become pregnant at some point during their college careers.[3] Another study says that 61% of students who have a child after enrolling in a community college drop out before finishing a degree.[4] Essentially, if you get pregnant and have a child while still in college, it is incredibly more difficult to complete your degree. No girl thinks that she will get pregnant, and no guy thinks he will get a girl pregnant. But it happens far too often.

emotional baggage

STDs and pregnancy are outcomes that you can measure, but the emotional baggage that lies beneath the surface can be much more difficult to identify. You can't measure guilt, regret, lowered self-esteem, and the emotional scars that are left behind from premarital sex. But realize those things are as real as pregnancy and disease. Some studies suggest that engaging in premarital sex often leads to depression and increased chance of suicide.[5] Plus, the fact that premarital sex is also likely to lead to promiscuity and future divorce.

---

[1] http://www.nursingschools.net/blog/2010/05/10-truly-shocking-stats-on-stds-and-college-students/
[2] http://www.leaderu.com/everystudent/sex/misc/stats.html
[3] http://youngadults.about.com/od/healthandsafety/qt/teenpregnancy.htm
[4] http://www.insidehighered.com/news/2009/11/25/pregnancy
[5] http://www.frc.org/get.cfm?i=IS06B01

I understand that you've probably heard this lecture before. Maybe you've heard some of these stats and facts before, or maybe it is brand new information. But the fact is that you don't think about these things in the heat of the moment. If you think it couldn't happen to you, or that these statistics don't apply to your world, you're kidding yourself. Instead of being naïve and assuming you'll be fine, you would be wise to think these things through now before you're in a situation, where you may not use your best judgment. Although I don't know of any formal study on the subject, my guess would be that if you asked students who had experienced a pregnancy, contracted an STD, or carried around emotional scars from a sexual relationship, I would bet that nearly 100% thought it wouldn't happen to them. We all think we're immune until the statistic becomes a reality.

If you're in a relationship, remember that you should never be pressured into doing anything you're not comfortable with. That doesn't make you a prude. That doesn't make you less popular. It just means that you have a backbone and are willing to stand up for something you believe in. If you're in a relationship, and the other person is pressuring you to do something you don't want to do, that is not a relationship you need to be in. Some people can be extremely controlling and manipulative in a relationship, and that's not healthy for either of you.

Let me make a disclaimer here to wrap up this chapter. Waiting to have sex until you are married is extremely difficult. You have all of these emotions and hormones raging through your body, and you feel like this caged animal just waiting for your moment to break free! I know, I know, I get it. But the principle we've discussed throughout this chapter is a principle that will serve you well in many other areas of life. You have got to learn how to delay gratification. Society pushes you to experience instant gratification, but waiting to have sex until you're married is worth the wait. I know because I did. My wife and I dated for five years, and we didn't have sex until we were married. Was it easy? Heck no! She's really hot! But was it worth it to wait? Absolutely.

chapter nineteen

this relationship is getting serious…what do I do?

It was just yesterday that you saw him in your English 101 class and thought he was kind of cute. Then through your network of friends and some Facebook stalking, rumors were swirling that he kind of liked you, and that he might even ask you out. A few days later that moment arrived.

Your eyes met through the sea of students and then, as if completely unscripted, "Endless Love" started playing over the intercom speakers (strange, I know). You took it as a sign, and started walking towards him. You made some small talk, and then it happened. He asked you out on a date. Sure it was just to McDonald's, and he made you share a #4 combo meal (in his defense, he did super-size it), but you were together. At least that's what you told yourself.

That first date was such a rush of emotion, wasn't it? You found out you liked each other, you had a lot in common, and somehow during that first date, you found yourself talking about how much you liked his hair. For the first few weeks of this new relationship, it all seemed like this fairy tale, made-for-Disney story. You talked on the phone all the time. You spent every waking moment together. And before long, what began as this flirty, fun little relationship starts evolving into something you hadn't expected it to become. It started getting…serious…(cue scary music) dum, dum, dum. So what do you do now?

As a relationship begins to get more and more serious, often times there is a sense of nervousness and anxiety that starts to set in. That is natural, so don't be alarmed. But at the same time, there's a reason that brain of yours is setting off signal flares to get your attention. When that relationship starts getting a little more serious, here are some things to consider:

don't panic

It's funny how sometimes we start getting really nervous when a relationship starts becoming serious. But let me ask you: what did you think was going to happen?! When a couple has been together for a significant period of time, it is just natural that long-term thinking begins to enter the equation. Thoughts start racing through your mind that maybe, just maybe, this is "The One." Perhaps you have stumbled upon that one, true soul mate that was destined for you, and he/she just happened to be in your Tuesday/Thursday Psych class. Anytime you have these thoughts flooding into your mind, it can cause you to panic! But remain calm. When you start panicking, it can lead to poor judgment and stupid decisions.

slow down

When it comes to a relationship, here's a simple principle to live by: it is better to go slow and get it right, than to speed it up and get it wrong. As a relationship begins to get more and more serious, it can become this small, innocent snowball that starts rolling down the hill. But next thing you know, it turns into an avalanche of destruction that is impossible to stop. The best thing you can do with a relationship that is starting to get serious is to slow down. Regardless of what you may think, time only helps strengthen relationships. When you slow down and remind yourself that there is no rush, you make better decisions and avoid moments of stupidity. My wife and I started dating in high school and got married on our five year anniversary. Five years we dated! And you know what? I wouldn't change a thing about it. That extra time allowed us to not only get to know each other better, but also to allow our relationship to develop a solid foundation.

ask the tough questions

When you've been together with someone for a while and things begin to get serious, it is time to start asking the tough questions. What brought you two together in the first place (attraction) will not be enough to sustain a relationship for the long haul. Enjoy that gorgeous hair he has now, because someday it's going to fall out! You have to take the time to ask the difficult questions about your individual goals, dreams, future plans, attitudes, integrity, etc. What does that other person plan on doing with the next five years of their life? How does that compare with what you want to do in that time? What do they want to be when they grow up? Are they "growing up" now, or are they still young and immature? Do you enjoy being with them, or do you constantly bicker and fight? Is this someone you want to spend your life with, or is this just a fun, cute relationship that has no potential for the future? Ask the difficult questions to evaluate not only where you are, but also where you see this going.

get feedback

When you're in a serious relationship, it can be very easy for your judgment to become clouded. It is like having "love glasses" on that fog your vision to what your relationship and that person may really be like. You may feel like it is you two against the world, but you would be ignorant to ignore the opinions and advice of others. While you may tend to see only the good in someone, the rest of your family and friends may think you're blind to what a loser he is! Be honest with others, and get feedback from your parents, trusted friends, and people whose opinion you value and respect. It may confirm that the relationship is a good thing, but on the other hand, they may see red flags in the other person or the relationship that you have missed. Not only should you ask for feedback, but be open-minded enough to listen and take it seriously. Reverse the scenario and ask yourself, if your best friend was in the same relationship you're in, what advice would you give them?

After asking the difficult questions and getting some honest feedback from others, what happens if you find yourself thinking that maybe this isn't the right relationship for you? Don't dilly-dally around if you're in an unhealthy relationship. You need to make a decision and move on.

chapter twenty
when will I be ready for marriage?

Whenever you've been dating someone for a fair amount of time, the subject of marriage inevitably comes up. Sometimes your friends begin asking the questions about how serious the relationship is. Of course your mom wants to know what's going on! Or maybe your girlfriend just comes right out and asks when she will be getting a ring! That's a scary and exciting feeling when you get to a point in a relationship where you are beginning to consider this person as marriage material. How do you know if you personally, and together as a couple, are ready for marriage? Consider these questions:

are you on the same page?

Author Dave Ramsey, says that before you get married, you should be in agreement on four big areas: money, religion, in-laws, and kids. Think about it. These are some of the biggest, hot-button issues in relationships. As it relates to money, are you a spender or a saver? What if you have completely different religious views and beliefs? What if your significant other wants to live next door to their parents? If you want one kid, and they believe kids are cheaper by the dozen, then you're going to have issues! If you haven't addressed these subjects with the person you're dating, then you're not ready for marriage.

is it the right time?

The right thing at the wrong time is still the wrong thing. It happens all too often that boy meets girl, they go on a couple of dates, and then start planning to be married within a few months. I don't think that is smart at all. So when is the right time? While every couple and every situation is different, I think you should date at least one year before you get engaged or consider getting married. My wife and I dated for five years, although some of that was while we were in high school. I've heard it said you should date through all four seasons before getting married (unless you live in San Diego in which case there is one season). But the more time you have with someone, the more you get to know them beyond the initial infatuation stage of a relationship. If it takes a baby nine months to develop and grow, it should take a relationship at least that long!

are you ready?

Let me go ahead and state the obvious: marriage is a lifelong commitment. Unfortunately in our culture, many people view marriage as this: "If it doesn't work out, it's no big deal, we'll just get a divorce." But nobody goes into a marriage planning to get a divorce. At least not normal, sane people. Marriage changes everything about your priorities. No longer is it about you. There is now this other person that you must be willing to die for. Whenever you get married, the minister reminds you this is for better or worse, in sickness and in health, and for richer or poorer…or really, really poorer (that's what the first few years of marriage are like!). Marriage doesn't work only when it is convenient for you. Because it is such a major commitment, you have to evaluate: Are you ready?

If you've been in a relationship for a long period of time and you don't plan on getting married, then I have to ask the question, what's the point? Part of the purpose of dating is so you can determine if this is someone that you want to spend the rest of your life with. If it's not, then you should be honest and caring enough for yourself and the other person to move on from the relationship. There is no sense in misleading someone or giving them the wrong impression about how you see the future of the relationship. Guys, don't lead girls on. That's not cool. And girls, the same goes for you. Don't play around with a guy's feelings. We're fragile.

The right thing at the wrong time is still the wrong thing.

section three

finances

chapter twenty-one
as a college student, how can I earn money?

Let's start by debunking the myth that you can't take a full load of classes and have a job. That's bologna. As in, Oscar Mayer wiener bologna. If you have a job and take classes, you will certainly be busy, but it is manageable. You will survive.

So why would you need a job in college? You're on your own now, so you will naturally have more expenses. And I assume you want to have a life right? As I'm sure you've figured out by now, having a life typically requires some cash. In which case, you'll be needing an income.

Very simply, there are two primary ways to earn money: work for someone else or work for yourself. The simplest and quickest way to start making money is to get a job. As you look for a job, it's easy to create a checklist defining your perfect position.

"I need a corner office. I want to work with my friends. I don't work nights or weekends or days that end in 'Y'. I want to wear shorts to work. I want my own parking spot. I want a Moon Bounce in the break room. I'd like a raise every other week. I need a 401k, health benefits, and an assistant. And I only want to work four hours a week (thank you Tim Ferriss)."

Ok, so maybe you're not to that extreme, but I'd guess you have a mental list of jobs you would or would not be willing to do. Here are things to remember though...

You just need a paycheck, so you can't afford to be picky.

You're not making a career decision here. Most likely, this isn't some move that will advance your career in anyway. Your job delivering pizzas won't lead to a job with Google. As long as they pay you in US currency and give you the number of hours you need and want, you're good to go.

If your job is not ideal, remember it's only temporary.

I know it's not what you want to do. I know you hate your boss and your co-workers and the customers are all jerks. But you won't be there for the rest of your life. Hang in there. Every adult has at one time or another had a job they hated. But as long as they still pay you, you can put up with it for a semester or two.

In order to find a job, you want to get the word out that you're looking. Most jobs are hired through word of mouth and are never even posted anywhere. Talk to friends and family. Check with area businesses you frequent. Post something on Facebook or Twitter. Put it on people's radars that you're in the market for a job. That way when an opportunity opens up, people will think of you.

Keep in mind though that some businesses may feel sketchy about hiring college students. Why? Because the mental image of a stereotypical college student doesn't exactly paint a picture of a responsible, hard-working, beacon-of-light employee. Therefore, you've got to make a good impression and prove you're the opposite of the stereotypical college student.

So while finding a part-time job may be the simplest and quickest way to start earning some money, you can also create your own income. As an entrepreneur, I'm a huge fan of students doing their own thing and starting a business. Sometimes the idea of starting a business seems intimidating and overwhelming. But we're not talking about creating some international corporate giant with plans to take over the world ala

Pinky and the Brain. We're talking about some simple ways to earn a few extra bucks on your own.

While there are countless small business ideas for college students, you really need one of two things: a product or a service. The options of what people will pay for is truly limitless. You could sell cupcakes or pies, re-sell name brand clothes, sell stuff on eBay or Craigslist, or design and sell t-shirts. You could offer services such as photography, web design, graphic design, tutoring, dorm/apartment cleaning, computer/tech support, or provide an errand service. If you search online, you can find thousands of ideas that fit what you may be looking for. If the idea of starting a business appeals to you, we'll talk more about it in Chapter 39.

Here's the nutshell of this chapter: do what you have to do, so you can do what you want to do. What is it that you want to do? I assume hang out with friends, be able to buy stuff you want, and in general have a life. In order to do/have that, you must do what you have to do. My dad used to always say, "work comes before play." Work hard, so you can play hard. On the playground. At college.

chapter twenty-two
how do I make better decisions with my money?

Unfortunately, managing your money is one subject that students may need the most knowledge in life, but get the least amount of training. I can't stress to you enough how important it is to take steps now, regardless of your age or where you're at in life, to learn how to handle money. Money (or the lack of it) can become one of the biggest stresses in life if you're not careful. So let's jump into this, and look at six things you have to do if you're going to learn how to manage your money:

create a game plan

In order to win with money, you have to know how much you have coming in and how much you have going out. You need to know where your money is going, so it doesn't just walk out of your wallet, as it may be doing now. In order to do all of this and effectively manage your money, you need a game plan. This is more commonly known as the dreaded "B" word. Not that "B" word, you filthy animal. Get your head out of the gutter. I'm talking about making a *budget* (cue scary music, screams, lightning, thunder, etc.). I'm going to talk more on the specifics of making a budget in the next chapter, but you need to know this…you have to have one! A budget is essentially a road map for handling your money. If you were going on a road trip, you would take the time to map out on Google or Map Quest where you were going and how you needed to get there. A budget is the same thing for your money. You have to have a game plan, otherwise you'll always end up with more month than money (figure that out!).

plan for rainy days

You have to plan for emergencies, because they will happen. It is not a matter of if it is going to rain, but rather when it does rain, do you have an umbrella? In case you haven't noticed, life happens. That's just the way it goes. So if you know it is going to rain, and you are going to have emergencies pop up in your life, wouldn't it just be smart to plan for them? If you plan for life's surprises, then it's no longer a big emergency, is it? Now it is more of an inconvenience, which is a pain, but it isn't that big of a deal. Think of the rainy days that happen in life: your transmission goes out on your car, your college textbooks get stolen, you end up in the hospital for a few days, or your apartment blows up (that's really bad). Those are the things that you think will never happen to you and yet when they do, you're up a creek.

For most students, I would recommend having a rainy day/emergency fund of $500 but preferably $1,000. For some of you, that may seem like a million dollars, and for others, you may think that is no big deal. But having $500 in the bank will catch the majority of emergencies that will come up in your world. This money should be put in a savings account, and should never be used unless it is an emergency. Spring Break in Cancun is not an emergency. Christmas is not an emergency. It is always on the same day in December. They don't move it. If you know it is coming, you should plan for it.

avoid debt like the plague

I'm talking about all kinds of debt...credit card debt, school loans, car loans, any type of debt...avoid it at all costs. Unfortunately, most Americans accept debt as a way of life. They say, "I'm always going to have a car payment." Or "I'm always going to have a credit card balance." That's stupid. If you can't pay cash for it, wait and save up until you can. Again, it goes back to that idea of delayed gratification. There's no sense in going into debt for some electronic gadget, a new outfit, or to go to the movies. Pay cash or don't get it. If you currently have debt, the only way you're ever going to get out of debt is to stop borrowing money. Imagine you were stuck in a hole. You really wanted to get out, but for whatever reason, every month you decided to dig down a few more feet, and make the hole just a little bigger. That's ridiculous. Quit borrowing money!

save like crazy

We are going to talk more about this in a later chapter, but you will quickly learn the power of compound interest. Wouldn't it be great if you started saving now, so you could be stinking rich when you're 40? What if you were so loaded that you could visit a store in the mall and just buy the entire store? Or maybe even the entire mall. That would be fun, wouldn't it? But again, that means delaying gratification now, so you can win later.

think long-term

Do you remember the story about the tortoise and the hare? More importantly, do you remember who came out on top? The way I remember it, the tortoise always wins the race. If you learn to make sacrifices today, it will always pay off in the long-term. Personal finance is 80% behavior and 20% head knowledge. I can give you the knowledge you need, but it really comes down to changing your behaviors and applying the things you read in this book to life in the real world.

give it away

It may sound strange, but one of the best things you can do with money is give it away. Weird, I know. But think about a time when you gave someone a gift, and you knew it really meant a lot to them. You put so much effort and thought into the present that to see their reaction was worth it all. At the risk of sounding like a Hallmark card, you really can't put a price on that feeling. When you've been smart with your money, you then have the ability, the opportunity, and maybe even the responsibility to help others. In addition, giving puts money in the proper perspective. There's nothing wrong with having new or nice things, but if that's what your life is all about, you've missed the point. When you give to other less fortunate, you realize the stuff you think you can't live without really isn't that big of a deal.

I know, I know. You're thinking all of these ideas look great on paper, but in real life, they are pretty difficult to carry out. It is true that managing your money isn't that difficult, but many people are convinced they can't do it. So they come up with excuses about money management when really they are just lazy! You can do each and every one of these things listed. Is it easy? Not necessarily. Is it worth it? Absolutely! I can say this because I've been on both sides of the coin.

Coming out of college, my wife and I had nearly $25,000 in debt. Car debt, credit cards, school loans…you name it, we had it. But we have followed these principles for handling and managing our money and today, we are debt-free except for our house. No more credit card debt. No car payments. No school bills. And do you know how that feels? To say it feels "really good" is a massive understatement. Instead of sending our money to all of these other people in the form of payments, now we get to keep it for ourselves, and do with it as we please. That is a great feeling of freedom, both personally and financially.

chapter twenty-three
is it okay to splurge on myself?

Picture this…you go to the mall with some friends planning to spend $50 on some new clothes. You browse around for a while until you find this pair of jeans that that is perfect for you. Oddly enough, there is only one pair left, and it happens to be in your size. It's almost too good to be true, but there's only one problem. They cost $100; twice as much as you had planned to spend, right? You justify that it's still a great deal, and you rationalize that you just can't live without them! "I deserve it," you tell yourself. You work hard, so you should get to spend a little extra on yourself, shouldn't you? Of course you should.

On top of that, as you are walking up to pay for your "twice-as-much-as-you-should-spend" pair of jeans, you notice a shirt that would perfectly complete this outfit! It is on sale for only $35. What's another $35, right? Of course, at the counter you find a watch and a necklace that match your newly created outfit, and eventually you leave the store having spent way more than you expected. But you deserve it, right?!

If you don't have the money, you don't deserve it!

Now you may get a little laugh out of this story, but don't kid yourself… this happens every day with college students just like you. You work hard all week between classes and a job, so it's easy to justify that we deserve to splurge a little on ourselves. It's our money, and we earned it, so we should be able to spend it how we want. But if you're not careful, you can very quickly waste a lot of money and rack up a lot of debt buying crap you don't need, all the while justifying how you deserve it.

So can you splurge on yourself a little? The simple answer is 'yes' and 'no'. Being able to splurge a little on yourself means something different to everyone. To one person, it may mean that instead of just getting a hamburger, you get the whole value meal! To someone else, splurging may mean that instead of buying one outfit, you buy the entire store! Obviously, there is a huge difference in how people view splurging. Basically, if you have the money and you want to spend a little on yourself within reason, there is nothing wrong with that…if you have the money. But it is absolutely stupid to splurge on yourself with money you don't have, by putting something on a credit card. There are so many people in our culture who try to live a *Steak and Lobster Lifestyle* on a *McDonald's Budget!* That doesn't work. You have to learn to live within your means. Here are three simple principles to help you do this:

don't splurge if you have debt

If you're in debt with car loans, school loans, or credit card debt, then now is not the time to be splurging. You've already created a mess, so why would you want to add to it? If you have any kind of debt, learn to delay gratification, make sacrifices, and you'll win long-term. Which is more valuable? A quick spring break trip to Cancun today or having the ability to take several weeks of vacation anywhere in the world tomorrow? Dave Ramsey, a financial guru, always says, "If you live like no one else, later you will get to live like no one else." Chew on that.

if you are going to splurge, splurge proportionally to your finances

If you're a greeter at Walmart (which would be an awesome job), and you make minimum wage, you probably can't afford to be taking ski trips to Switzerland! If you're going to splurge on something, it has to make sense for your finances. If you make $1,000 a month and you want to blow $200 on clothes, that's 20% of your income. But if you make $10,000 a month and you want to blow $200 on clothes, that's only 2% of your income. Which makes more sense?

splurging only produces a temporary feeling

For some people, the danger in splurging is that it produces a type of euphoric buzz. There is a certain rush of adrenaline and excitement when you buy a really nice outfit or eat at an ultra fancy restaurant. But remember, that is just temporary. If you're thinking about splurging on something, sleep on it, wait 24 hours, and then ask yourself if you really need it. This can help prevent you from making stupid decisions.

Let me stress one other key point here. What you spend your money on doesn't define who you are. If you need to, stop, go back, and reread that statement. What you spend your money on doesn't define who you are. I don't care how expensive your clothes are, how big your house is, what kind of car you drive, or how much money you make. All of those things are trivial compared to who you are as a person. If you catch anything from this chapter, make it this: don't splurge on crap just to impress other people. That is immature, shallow, and stupid. Chances are, the people who try to impress others with how they spend their money are probably in so much debt, they can't see the light of day. Don't be that person.

chapter twenty-four
do I still need a budget if I'm broke?

Whether you make millions of dollars or just tens of dollars, you need a budget. My guess is because you're human, you're really good at spending money, yes? Me too. We all are. For everyone who is breathing, the default mode for handling money is to spend it. Since I can assume you're really good at spending money, I'd also be willing to bet that at some point you've: a) spent money on something you didn't need, and/or b) spent money but had no idea what you spent it on.

Again, we've all done that. Welcome to the club. I'm the President.

Leadership author and expert John Maxwell said, "A budget is telling your money where to go instead of wondering where it went." Bingo.

Think of it like a map for a road trip. If we were going to pile in the car and take a road trip, the first thing we need is some directions. We could use GPS or Google Maps, but we would need something to help get us from where we are to where we want to be. Once we have a map, it takes the stress out of knowing which exit to take or which highway to get on. You just follow the directions. The same thing is true with money. Most of us aren't sure about how to spend/save/handle our money, because we don't have any map. A budget is that guide.

Part of the value of starting to budget now while in college even if you don't have a ton of money is you're creating a habit. If you don't budget when you make $100 per month, why would you budget when you earn $10,000 per month? You want to begin establishing these financial habits that will stick with you for the rest of life.

So we understand that a budget is important, but how do you actually create one? Here are some tips and tricks:

write it down

Most of us like to think we have a budget in our head. But really how safe is any information in your head? Most of us can't even remember what we ate for breakfast yesterday (was it Fruity Pebbles or that Pop Tart?). Why trust your A.D.D. brain when you can simply put it on paper? Part of the value of writing it down is to create a visual goal for yourself. When it's in your head, you can randomly adjust based on your present circumstances, but when it's written down, it tends to be taken more seriously. According to a Harvard study, graduates found that after two years, the 3% who had written down their goals achieved more financially than the other 97% combined! Writing down your goals matters.

make a new budget every month

Sometimes we think we can make this error-free budget from heaven that will work on any given month. But you know there's no such thing as a perfect month. Your income and expenses will almost always vary, and that is something you have to plan for. Your income is different in July (summer, free time, full-time job) versus in September (classes starting, part-time job). Your expenses in June (living at home with Mom) will be different than December (Christmas, travel, candy canes). Every month is different, so you need to plan accordingly.

use the envelope system

The envelope system is a process in which you pay for as much stuff as possible in cash. Here's how it works. The first thing you do is determine common expenses that you can pay for in cash. These are categories such as groceries, gas, entertainment, clothing, restaurants, etc. Once you have set up your budget, and you know what the amounts are for each of these categories, go through and withdrawal the budgeted amount in cash from your checking account, and stick each amount in its own envelope. This is a way to force yourself to budget. When you need to buy groceries, you take money from the grocery envelope and spend only that. Any change left over goes back into the grocery envelope. If you only have $20 in your grocery envelope, and it's only the first week of the month, you're going to be eating a lot of Ramen noodles!

Think about why this works so well. Let's say you go to the mall and pay for your purchases with a debit card. You've made a budget, and you know you have $50 to spend, so you've picked out $50 worth of stuff to buy. But as you're walking up to pay, you notice a great shirt that's on sale for only $10. Ten bucks! No big deal, so you go ahead and add it to the pile, and your total comes to around $60. You know you're $10 over, but what's the big deal? But what if you used the envelope system and paid for your items in cash…guess what? If you walk into the mall with just a $50 bill, you're not leaving with $60 worth of stuff unless you want to spend the night in the slammer with Bubba and Rico.

My wife and I have used this system for five years now, and I'll tell you…it works! You are forced to pay attention to where your money is going, and how you are spending it. On top of that, when you pay for something in cash, it is more difficult than just swiping a card. If I go to the grocery store, and my tab is $100, it is much more difficult to hand the cashier a crisp $100 bill that I earned, as opposed to just swiping a piece of plastic that I don't have to think about. At least try the envelope system for a couple of months, and if you don't like it, then you can go back to your system: being broke!

I can't stress this enough: If you want to win with money, you've got to make a budget. Every month. Accounting for every dollar. You absolutely must do it. The first few times you make a budget, it may be a complete disaster. But I promise you, if you work at it and stick to your road map, each month you make a budget will be a little easier than the previous. Before long, you'll be able to do a budget in your sleep. And when *that* happens, you've entered the final level as a Budget Jedi Master. Congratulations.

chapter twenty-five
do I need to get a credit card?

Quite honestly, a credit card is probably not the best thing for a student to have, especially a student with no money! This means pretty much all students, then, since they're usually all broke! While I don't think that credit cards are inherently evil, I don't think they're a good idea for most people. When you look at credit cards as a whole, you will find that the bad far outweighs the good.

For example, did you know that the average credit card debt per household with credit card debt is $15,799 with an average interest rate around 14%![1] That amounts to $2,359 a year in interest payments. Think of this: if you took that $2,359 that you pay in just interest alone and invested that over a 40 year period with a 12% average return, you would end up with over $2.3 million!

Our society thinks debt is just a part of life. Culture expects you will always have a car loan, credit card bill, or a student loan payment. They tell you once you get into debt, there's nothing you can do – you're just stuck there

---

[1] http://www.creditcards.com/credit-card-news/credit-card-industry-facts-personal-debt-statistics-1276.php

forever. That's the stupidest thing I've ever heard. If you think you have to have a credit card, let me at least give you a few things to consider:

high interest rates

Credit cards are known to have some of the highest and most ridiculous interest rates of any type of lender. Seventy-two percent of credit cards have a variable interest rate, meaning your interest rate can change on a regular basis. Also, because you're younger with less credit history to back you up and therefore a bigger risk, you're more likely to have an interest rate between 25%-30%. Plus, virtually all credit cards today have a provision in the contract that essentially says they can raise your interest rate at any time, for any reason, without warning.

"gotcha" fees

Credit cards have all kinds of ridiculous fees for just about anything and everything you can think of. They can gouge you if you're a day late on your payment or if you spend more than your credit limit. These fees can be anywhere from $20 to as much as $50. With some cards, there are also transaction fees for calling the "toll-free" number to check your balance and penalty fees if you haven't used your card in awhile and your account has been inactive. In a study done by Georgetown University, they found that college students tend to make late payments and exceed their credit limits more frequently than other age groups and therefore incur more fees than other groups. [1]

emotional strain

Any time you have debt, it feels like a big weight you carry around. In a very real sense, you are a slave to whomever you owe that money to. Every time you collect a paycheck, a good chunk of that money is going to pay your debt; you always end up working for someone else as opposed to working for yourself. A study by the American Bankruptcy Institute reveals that 19% of the people who filed for bankruptcy last year were college students, and

---

[1] http://www.money-zine.com/Financial-Planning/Debt-Consolidation/Credit-Card-Debt-Statistics

that 69% of bankruptcy filers said credit card debt caused the bankruptcy. Never underestimate the emotional and mental toll that debt will have on your life.

When it comes to the dangers of credit cards, most people will have one of these common responses for why they need a credit card:

"it's only for emergencies"

This is why we mentioned earlier that you have to create an emergency fund. If you have a rainy day fund in place, there is no need to have a credit card for emergencies.

"I pay it off each month"

According to CardTrak.com, 60% of people don't pay off their credit cards every month. Which makes me wonder…do you think that the 60% of people who don't pay off their cards had the same idea as you? They probably thought they would just pay it off each month, too – no big deal. Until life happened. And they were late a day, and the credit card company tacked on a nice little fee they hadn't planned on. Or they lost track of how much they put on the card that month and when the bill came, they only paid the minimum payment. This is far too common. On top of that, a study by Dunn & Bradstreet shows that credit card users spend 12%-18% more when using credit instead of cash. Paying off your credit card balance each month sounds nice in theory, but it doesn't always work like you plan.

While I think credit cards do bring a lot of risks especially to college students, in full disclosure I will say that I have and use a business credit card. Because I travel a lot for business, I use a credit card for travel expenses to earn additional airline miles that I use frequently. If you are going to have a credit card, here are three rules to follow (I follow all these rules for my own credit card purchases):

keep a low credit limit

Your credit limit is the maximum amount a credit card company will allow you to charge before they ding you with a fee. The bigger that credit limit, the more likely you'll spend up to that amount. Keep a low credit limit around $500-$1,000.

pay it off every month

When you pay off your card every month, you won't be charged any interest. You can't really view it like free money though, since you still have to pay it back. To take this rule a step further, the first month you can't pay off the balance, cut up the card. When you get to a place where you're only making minimum payments to get by, you're on a slippery slope that leads to nowhere good financially.

only use for budgeted purchases

Don't use your credit card for random, splurge expenses. Bad idea. If you've got $300 budgeted to buy your family Christmas presents, there's nothing wrong with putting that $300 in charges on your card. Again, as long as you're paying it off that month and you use the $300 that was allotted in your budget, you're fine.

You have to decide for yourself if you're responsible enough to have a credit card. If you are going to have one, establish some ground rules for yourself BEFORE you get the card, and then follow your self-imposed rules religiously.

chapter twenty-six
how do I build my credit score?

You may have heard this before or even asked yourself this question, but the idea that you need to "build credit" is really kind of silly when you think about it. When people say they need to "build credit," they are referring to their credit score, which is also known as the FICO score. Your credit score is a three-digit number that serves as a measurement for banks, credit card companies, and other lending organizations to help them determine how reliable you will be to pay back money you borrow. The higher your score, the more likely you will be to pay back money you owe. If you have a lower score, it may mean that you paid a bill late in the past, perhaps you've filed for bankruptcy, or maybe you owe some money that you never even bothered to repay. Here is a breakdown for how your credit score is figured:

- 35% payment history
- 30% amount of debt
- 15% length of credit history
- 10% type of debt
- 10% applying for new credit

If you look through each of these factors that combine to make up your credit score, they all have one thing in common: DEBT! Your credit score is all based on how well you can borrow money and pay it back. It is a score based on how much you love debt! Are you beginning to see how stupid this seems? So if you have a salary of $5 million per year, no debt, and $20 million in the bank, you may have a low credit score simply because you are debt free. So in reality, the higher your credit score, the better you are at acquiring and repaying debt. Is that really what you want to be financially known for?

If you've been paying attention to anything you've read in this section so far, you probably picked up on the fact that if you want to succeed financially, you've got to learn to stay out of debt. Having a good credit score is NOT an indication of wealth or success. Some of the richest people in America say the key to wealth is living debt free. This means their credit scores probably suck! Hopefully, you're beginning to see that a crappy credit score may be a good thing!

You may wonder then how you buy a car or a house. If you need to buy a car, you need to be diligent enough to save up and pay cash for it. This is what my wife and I do, and we have never regretted it. Let's be honest though, if you're paying cash for a car, that probably means you don't have enough saved to get a really nice car. Just start with what you can afford, then continue to save up and upgrade your car every few years. That's exactly what we do. Our first mini-van (that's right, I rock a mini-van) was junk. But it's what we could afford at the time. We continued to save and have upgraded a few times since then to a pretty nice van now. And the best part? We paid cash along the way.

I will admit that a house is a little different monster. Ideally, it would be great if you could save up and pay cash for a house, but I'm realistic enough to know that most people, especially young adults in their twenties, would have a tough time pulling this off. If you need to get a loan for a house, there are ways to get one without needing a credit score. You will have to go to a mortgage company or lender that does what is called *manual underwriting*. This is when a lender looks at you, as an individual, to make a decision about lending you money for a mortgage, as opposed to making a lending decision based solely on a three-digit number (which any monkey could do!). If you are considering *manual underwriting*, here are some common factors lenders will look at to determine if you qualify for a mortgage:

- You have paid your landlord early or on time for two years.
- You have no other credit or debt.
- You have a solid down payment – nothing down is not solid. You really want to have 10%-20%.
- You have been in the same career field for two years.
- You are not trying to bite off more than you can chew. Your payment on your mortgage should be around 25% of your take-home pay. If you make $2,000 a month and request a loan with a payment of $1,200 month…good luck.

As you have probably figured out, lenders want to see that you are a stable, normal person, and that you're not going to wig out on them. In reality, if you can still qualify for a mortgage without a credit score, and if you plan on paying for everything else in cash, then I guess that defeats the purpose of trying to build your credit score, doesn't it?

chapter twenty-seven
do I really have to pay taxes?

As you may have already discovered, and will continue to learn as you get older, taxes are a necessary evil! You might as well get used to the government always taking a chunk of the money you make! It's a bummer in life: the more money you make, the more they take.

Welcome to the real world. Not always so fun, is it?!

If you're in college working a part-time job, you probably realize that you're already paying income taxes whether you like it or not. Every time you get a paycheck from your employer, you've noticed there are large chunks of money missing from your check. Why? Very simply, the government wants their cut before you get yours. If you've had a job for over a year and have filed taxes, you've probably also noticed that most of the money the government takes is given back to you at the end of the year. Effective system, huh?!

The nutshell of taxes is this: in order to keep functioning, the government collects taxes in a variety of different forms. If you go to the store and buy something, you know you're going to pay sales tax on your purchase. At the same time, if you have a job, the government will withhold income tax from you. Of course, we all hate how much money we pay to the government, but it is just part of life. You may as well make your peace with it now.

One thing you may have figured out by now is if you earn an income at all, you must file your income taxes for that year. When I say "file your taxes," that means once a year, you fill out some paperwork to tell the government how much money you made and how much you owe them. Like I mentioned before, your employer will take a little bit out of each paycheck throughout the year. This prevents you from having to pay a big chunk of taxes at the end of year. By the way, you must file your taxes each year by April 15 for your previous year's income. For example, if you were filing your taxes for the income you made in 2011, you must file those forms with the government by April 15, 2012.

Your income tax is based on how much money you make. If you're working at a part-time job, you will probably owe very little, if any, taxes at the end of the year. If your employer withheld your taxes from you, that amount will be given back when you file your taxes, which is known as a *refund*. As you get older and presumably make more money, the government will want a bigger and bigger piece of the pie. There are various federal tax brackets, so if you are single and make $25,000, your tax rate might be around 15%. But if you make $50,000, your tax rate could jump to closer to 25%. It is based on a sliding scale and again, will vary depending on your income. It's also important to note that federal tax rates are different than state tax rates, and some states collect no income tax at all.

One of the best things you can do now is be familiar with the process. If you're not a numbers person (or you have a headache after reading these first few paragraphs), then find someone to help you with your taxes. Make friends with an accounting major or a future CPA on campus who can help you out. Personally, I do my own taxes and have done so since I was a teenager. I have learned a lot in the process by doing them myself. Every year, I use a computer software program, which greatly simplifies the process. Of course you can always figure your taxes using just the tax form and a pencil.

If you do your taxes yourself, make certain you know what you're doing. The government doesn't mess around when it comes to taxes. They don't care if you're a naïve 18 year old who has never filed taxes before. They just want to know exactly what you earned, so they make sure they get a chunk of that money. If you're off by a penny, they may not throw you in jail tomorrow but just understand how important it is to file your taxes accurately. Regardless of what your personal feeling is about taxes, it is still your responsibility as an American to pay them. Be someone with integrity and honesty who doesn't try to cheat or cut corners on your taxes. Sure, no one may find out, but you know it's unethical, and that's not something you want to live with. As Benjamin Franklin once said, "In this world, nothing is certain but death and taxes." Ain't that the truth?

chapter twenty-eight
should I be saving money for retirement?

You don't need to stress about retirement right now, but it is a smart idea to begin thinking about it. It sounds overly simplistic, but if you begin preparing for the future now, you can retire as a very wealthy person! In fact, you will have a major advantage over your parents in planning for retirement, because you have one key element on your side:

time

In order to best utilize the time that is on your side, you have to apply one principle we've talked about throughout the book: delayed gratification. Instead of spending $20 now, wait several years, make smart decisions along the way, and it could be worth $200. However, given the choice between $20 now or $200 in several years, most students would probably take the cash now. Planning for retirement is about making smart decisions and being disciplined now, so you can win long-term. In order to utilize the time that is on your side, you have to understand a powerful principle that would make your math teacher very proud:

compound interest

Maybe you've heard of compound interest before, or maybe you skipped that day of school, but either way, it's a pretty simple concept. It is the idea of adding accumulated interest back to the original principal amount, so that you are earning interest on top of your interest. It's pretty cool when you think about it. You are essentially earning free money off of free money. I like it.

Here's a simple math example to show you what I mean. Let's say on your 18th birthday, you put $1,000 in an investment account, and you never deposited or withdrew anything from that account until age 65 when you retire. That's 47 years. Remember, just a one-time $1,000 investment that you never touch.

- At 6% interest per year (a nice savings bond), you would have just over $16,000 at age 65. Not bad for a $1,000 investment.

- At 12% interest per year (solid mutual funds), your total amount would jump to around $32,000, right? But in fact, you would have over $230,000!

- At 18% interest per year (real estate), that initial $1,000 deposit could end up making you a multi-millionaire. You could have about $2.8 million at age 65!

Now let's acknowledge a few things with this example. Is there any type of investment that will net you a guaranteed 18% every year? Probably not. The idea of turning a single $1,000 deposit into $2.8 million sounds a little more fantasy than reality. I can acknowledge that. But that's not the point. The point is the potential math and the difference that time and compound interest can make to the equation.

Now while each of these interest rates are realistic, the higher the interest rate, the greater the risk. You can get a 6% return on a savings bond with little to no risk, but getting 18% on a piece of real estate is going to be extremely risky. There are certainly pros and cons either way, and while the interest rates aren't necessarily the issue, I want you to understand the power of starting early.

Remember slow and steady wins the race. Here's one more example. Suppose you started at age 18 and saved for 47 years until age 65, saving only $50 per month at a 12% average annual return. Although you would have saved only around $29,000, at the end of 47 years you would have nearly $1.3 million, thanks to all the interest you earned. I know you could come up with $50 per month. Just stop eating so many Skittles and Twinkies. Boom. Problem solved.

Not to over-simplify it, but if you start now and are consistent in putting away money for retirement, you will be loaded with cash sooner than you think! But it takes delaying gratification today, so that you can win tomorrow. Again, it is important to determine what you want to do with the money in order to determine how best to invest it. Without getting too deep into investing, strategy, rates of return, and risk, here are a few principles for investing and saving money:

understand your investment

Don't put money into anything unless you know what it is. I don't care if your parents gave you investment advice, a stock broker told you about a can't-miss opportunity, or you got a hot stock tip from your dog. Don't put money into something unless you understand it. When it comes to investing for retirement, here are two of the most common retirement plans:

401(k)
This is a retirement plan that allows your place of employment to contribute to your investment. Companies that offer a 401(k) will generally match a certain percentage of your salary and contribute that to your investments. Basically, they're giving you free money for retirement. This is a good thing. A 401(k) is a tax-deferred account meaning any money you put in you don't pay taxes on. That's good today but all the money you take out at retirement (age 59½) will be taxed as income including all the growth on your investments.

Roth IRA
A Roth IRA is another retirement plan that anyone can set up. The biggest benefit to the Roth IRA is it uses after-tax dollars and grows tax free. So basically if you put in $1,000 today, you would pay taxes on that initial deposit. But if you take that money out when you're 65, and it's grown to be worth $10,000, you wouldn't pay any taxes on the $9,000 in growth. Pretty cool, huh? This makes the Roth extremely appealing to younger people, since although you pay taxes on your contributions now, all the growth that will take place over time comes out tax free.

Start by checking with your employer and see if they offer a 401(k) plan. You may need to have worked at the company for a certain length of time in order to qualify, but you don't know unless you ask. After you've maxed out your 401(k) and earned all the free money your company will contribute, a Roth IRA is going to be your best option.

have a plan

Always know why you're investing in something and stick to your plan. In addition to 401(k)'s and Roth IRAs, there are college savings plans (commonly called 529 Plans or Educational Savings Accounts – ESAs), money market accounts, savings accounts, and plenty of other options available for earning money on your money. Rather than just throwing it all in one big melting pot, have a plan for each dollar. My wife and I have several different savings accounts for various purposes. We have an emergency fund, two Roth IRAs, a separate investment account for retirement, a vacation savings account, college 529 accounts for each of our daughters, a savings fund for a new car, plus several more. Each account has a specific plan and purpose.

leave it alone

Don't invest in anything unless you are planning on leaving the money alone for at least five years. Otherwise you are just saving, not investing. When you have a long-term perspective on your investing, you don't get caught up in the hype of what the market is doing on a day-to-day basis. If you watch too much news, you get the impression that the sky is falling and we're all going to die. I have a lot of money invested in the stock market, but I probably couldn't tell you what happened in the market yesterday. And to be honest, I'm really not concerned about what happens tomorrow. Since I won't be touching that retirement money for another 30+ years, I'm confident that if tomorrow the market dips one direction or the other, it will correct itself over the next 30 years. Don't panic and start moving money around because of the media. Park it in something that has a long, solid track record, and then leave it alone. You can reunite in 30-40 years.

chapter twenty-nine
what do I need insurance for?

Like taxes, insurance is one of those necessary evils in life. You can feel like you're throwing money away with it, but if a disaster strikes, you're going to be real happy you have it. For the past number of years, you've probably been under your parents' various insurance policies, but all that is coming to an end. It is important to begin figuring out now, not only what insurance is, but why you need it, and what types of insurance you should have.

what is insurance?

When you purchase insurance, you pay money (known as a *premium*) to transfer risk from yourself to the insurance company. Let's take car insurance as an example. We all know that any time you get in a car and go for a drive, there is a chance you could get in an accident. The accident may be that an old lady behind you tapped your bumper or your car got hit by a train (you would rather deal with the old lady than the train). If you're in an accident, and it requires $5,000 worth of repairs to your car, chances are you don't have $5,000 lying around waiting to fix your damaged car. This is where insurance comes in. Instead of spending $5,000 out of your pocket to fix the car, you would have auto insurance which helps to protect you. You pay a monthly premium, and in exchange, the insurance company will help pay for damages if the car is in an accident. This is the basic idea of insurance.

One other key insurance term you need to be familiar with is a *deductible*. Very simply, a deductible is the amount you have to pay first (above your monthly premiums) before your insurance coverage will kick in and pay for damages. Going back to our example above, if you have a $1,000 deductible on your car insurance, you have to pay that amount first and the insurance company will cover everything above that related to the repairs. It's important to note that this differs from one insurance company to the next in terms of what they cover after you pay your deductible. Make sure you fully understand your insurance policy. When it comes to your deductible, there is a simple equation insurance companies use:

High Deductibles = Lower Premiums
AND
Low Deductibles = Higher Premiums

If your deductible is $500, your monthly premium may be much higher than if your deductible was $2,500. Remember that your monthly premium is based on risk. A brand new, 16-year-old driver is much more expensive to insure than a 45 year old who has never had a wreck. Obviously the 16 year old poses a much higher risk than the 45 year old, due to age and experience, so just remember that your premiums will be higher now than later. The opposite would be true with health insurance. A 45-year-old adult poses a greater health risk than an 19-year-old college freshmen, so health insurance is generally cheaper when you're younger.

do I need insurance?

You absolutely need and have got to have insurance. I know it's expensive. I know you're a great driver, and you have perfect health, so it seems like a waste of money, but you must have insurance. Insurance is there, not for the small fender bender or a runny nose, but to protect you from the major catastrophe you don't see coming. You may be in perfect health today, but if you're in a freak accident that puts you in the hospital for a week, you could easily have over $100,000 in medical bills. Do you have $100,000 in cash ready for those situations? I didn't think so! One study showed the number one cause of bankruptcy, accounting for half of the bankruptcies

---

[1] http://www.consumeraffairs.com/news04/2005/bankruptcy_study.html

in the US, was medical bills.[1] So yes, you must have insurance. Not for the little problems, but for the disastrous crisis that you least expect.

what kinds of insurance do I need?

You can get insurance coverage on just about anything, but here are a few types of insurance that everyone needs.

auto insurance
Insurance for your car is one type of insurance that isn't optional. In fact, it's the law. Like any other type of insurance, there are different types and variations of car insurance, but the bottom line is, in most states it is illegal to drive without car insurance.

health insurance
There's a chance you may still be covered under your parents' health insurance, but it would be a good idea to have them check at what age you will no longer be covered. Some policies cut you off at 18, others at 21, and still others may wait until you move out of the house. As we've stressed before, now that you're on your own, you've got to get health insurance. Check with your employer, because many companies offer some type of insurance that is generally cheaper than what you can get on your own.

renter's & life insurance
You may also look into renter's insurance (if you rent an apartment or a house) and life insurance (depending if you are married or have children). Find a reputable insurance agent in your area to discuss what types of insurance you need for your current situation.

Not to beat a dead horse (I wonder if the horse had life insurance?), but you have to make sure your bases are covered when it comes to insurance. If a disaster strikes in your life, you want to be prepared, and insurance is one way to make that happen.

chapter thirty

should I be concerned about identity theft?

Unless you've been living in a cave for the past several years (that would be cool…no pun intended), you've probably seen or heard something in the news about a growing problem known as identity theft. Whether you realize it or not, this is becoming a huge crisis in America, and it is certainly something you should be aware of. To start with, let's clarify exactly what identity theft is.

Basically, identity theft is when someone steals your personal information and pretends to be you, usually for financial gain. They can use this form of fraud in a variety of ways. They may use your personal information to open a new credit card account and charge it up, all while pretending to be you. They may gain access to your banking information and clean out your accounts. Identity theft can take several different forms, but the thing you need to realize is how common this has become. MSNBC reports that 1 in 12 people will become a victim of identity theft.

The biggest pain about identity theft is cleaning up the mess the thief left behind. If they have your personal information and pretend to be you, they will probably be charging up credit cards, opening new accounts and buying random junk. You're then stuck trying to convince all those places where the thief made purchases that it wasn't really you in the first place.

That's not my idea of a good time. A study shows that victims now spend an average of 600 hours recovering from this crime, which represents nearly $16,000 in lost potential income.[1]

So how does someone even go about stealing your identity? Identity theft generally starts with how you handle your personal information, such as your name, Social Security number, credit card numbers, or other financial account information. If an identity thief can get their hands on this info, they have hit the jackpot. You should also know that a high majority of identity theft cases involve a close friend or family member who may have easy access to your personal information. Other than family members, friends, or general misuse of your information, here are other ways that identity thieves work:

data theft

Since 2005, over 200 million people have had their identities stolen through corporate data theft. This happens when identity thieves gain access to customer records for major businesses and corporations. One example of data theft occurred when nearly 46 million identities were stolen from corporate giant, TJ Maxx.

stealing

Thieves are looking for anything where they can get your personal information. Wallets, purses, mail (especially bank and credit card statements), pre-approved credit offers, tax information, or even job and personnel records.

phishing

You may have encountered this online before; identity thieves pretending to be financial institutions or companies by sending spam or pop-up messages to get you to reveal your personal information. This is extremely common online, and you should always be heads up for this.

---

[1] http://www.zanderins.com/idtheft/stats.aspx

changing your address

Sometimes identity thieves will fill out a change of address form so that your personal mail starts getting directed to a new address. Then the thieves can begin collecting your mail and going through your personal information.

So how do you avoid this happening to you? Here are some ideas:

pay attention

The best thing you can do is just to keep an eye on your finances and your personal information for anything out of the ordinary. If anything suspicious happens such as missing checks from your checkbook, not receiving your bank or credit card statement in the mail, or getting a call from a collection agency about a charge you didn't make, a red flag should go off in your head.

be a shredding machine

Of course there are certain files and documents you must save, but for everything else, shred it. First of all, let's be honest...shredding stuff is really kind of fun. Don't deny it. If there is anything that has any personal information on it that you don't need to keep for any reason, shred it immediately. And enjoy!

be skeptical

If you get a random call from someone asking for your personal information, don't give it to them. If you get an email asking for personal data, delete the email. Don't roll the dice on something like identity theft.

If you ever think you are a victim of identity theft, there are several things you should do immediately:

file a police report

If someone stole your car, you would let the police know right away, wouldn't you? File a police report, and keep a copy of the report for your records.

check your credit report

Your credit report is a listing of your current debt and your debt history. There are three major credit bureaus that keep track of this: Experian[1], Equifax[2], and Trans Union.[3] If you notice anything suspicious on your credit report, you should put a fraud alert on your report. You can do this by going to the individual credit bureau websites.

cancel any suspicious accounts

If you think someone got your bank information, close that account and switch banks. Notify the bank or the organization, so they will be heads up to anything suspicious. If your purse or wallet is stolen, cancel any type of account or card immediately that a thief may then have access to. Also, put a *stop payment* on all lost or stolen checks and cards.

You don't need to live in fear everyday that someone will steal your identity, but you should be aware that it is just as likely to happen to you as it is to anyone else. Pay attention, be smart, and you should be fine. But even then, in the unlikely situation that your identity is stolen, do whatever you need to do to get the mess cleaned up immediately.

---

[1] www.experian.com
[2] www.equifax.com
[3] www.transunion.com

section four

beyond college

chapter thirty-one
school, work, activities, life… how do I balance it all?

Balancing everything that you have going on in life is a continual struggle. You have a limited amount of time, energy, and resources and an unlimited amount of opportunities where you can spend them. So how do you balance it all? Is it even realistic to have balance, or is it just a big myth? Here are some key ideas to keep in mind:

determine what matters most

As you are pulled in countless directions, you should begin to determine what matters most to you. Unless you determine your priorities, then suddenly everything is important and nothing is important all at the same time. One thing you might consider is creating a personal mission statement to help guide you. Companies and organizations have mission statements that help define who they are and what they are about. By having a personal mission statement, you can better define what matters and what doesn't in your life.

create boundaries

Here is a great word to add to your vocabulary that you need to start using frequently: "NO!" This is a word that you have to get good at using in order to maintain any sense of balance. If you create a mission statement, then you can use this as a tool to set boundaries in your life. Creating boundaries will give you the ability to say 'no' to the things that you just can't do.

you are not a machine

As young and active as we are (you more so than me), we still have our limits. If you work 60 hours a week, take a full load of classes, stay involved in all your clubs and activities, keep up with your homework, and try to have some friendships along the way, you are going to kill yourself. You have limits and a capacity to what you're capable of doing, so remind yourself of that when you think you're a machine.

stop and smell the roses

Life is too short to just work, work, work, and then fall over and die. I want to enjoy life along the way, don't you? That means you have to build in fun, recreation, and downtime along the way. Most students don't have a problem with this, but as you continue into the real world, it will become more and more difficult. Don't become too consumed with the busyness of life that you forget to stop and smell the roses.

who you are is more important than what you do

I use this phrase all the time, and I believe it whole-heartedly. Unfortunately though, we live in a culture that values possessions and titles over people. Think about when you first meet someone, what is one of the first questions you ask: "So, what do you do for a living?" And immediately people will make assumptions about you based solely on what you do. Whether you are the CEO or the janitor, who you are will always be more important than what you do.

balance doesn't naturally happen

As you may have figured out by now, balance doesn't just happen. It is something you have to be extremely proactive about working towards. There will always be opportunities to spend more time than what you have available. You have to set up those boundaries and determine what you are going to do differently. Think through some practical, proactive things you can do to begin to achieve balance in your own life.

This is one of the most important chapters in this book, because so few of us are good at balance. People work their entire lives to obtain status, fancy titles, nice things, and lots of money, but if your quality of life sucks and you are just a shell of human being, is it really worth it? That is no way to live. On your death bed someday, will you be concerned about what kind of car you drove or what brand your clothes were? Or will you be thinking about the memories you created with the people you love most? Make it a priority now to work towards balance.

chapter thirty-two
how do I create goals?

Creating and working towards goals are critical components of being successful in the future. Goals are a way for you to bring clarity and focus to where you're going in life. There's the old saying that "If you aim at nothing, you will hit it every time." There are three basic components to creating and carrying out your goals:

establish priorities

Before you can do anything, you have to determine what is most important to you. Once you have clarity on what your priorities are, then you can establish how that affects your time, your money, and everything else around you. It's important to realize that your priorities will be different from others. What's important to you may not be important to me. It's easy to get caught up living someone else's life because we try to mimic their priorities rather than establish our own. Also, recognize that your priorities may change over time. What's important to you now as a college student will be different in 20 years when you have a career and are possibly married with a family. The important thing, though, is for you to step back, evaluate your life, and really put down on paper what's important to you.

build goals around priorities

Once you have determined what your priorities are, then it's time to begin actually organizing your schedule and your life around those things. Begin to create a list of goals that are based on your priorities. Here's what I mean: If your family is your top priority, then what goals do you need to establish in order to reflect that? If school is your top priority, what goals will help you live that out? As you begin to create goals based on your priorities, here is an acroynm for the criteria your goals should meet – S.M.A.R.T. Goals:

specific
What is the exact result you want to achieve? Be as specific as possible. Goals like "I want to make more money" sound nice but are really vague. By answering specifically how much money you want to make, you can be more detailed when setting your goal. For example, you could say, "I want to make $10,000 in the next six months." That is a very specific, detailed goal.

measurable
What is a successful result? How will you know that you've reached your goal? For example, if I said "I want to have a closer relationship with my mom," that's good, but how do you measure that? How do you know if you're accomplishing it? Try to make it measurable which typically involves a number you can quantify. So instead you could say this, "I want to call my mom three times each week and have a meaningful 20 minute conversation." That you can measure. You can track how you're doing. You're working to accomplish the same objective as your original goal of "I want to have a closer relationship with my mom," but now you can measure it.

attainable
I'm all for dreaming big, but you have to ask yourself if your goal is realistic. "I want to fly to the moon by Thursday" – sounds good; it's even measurable and specific, but good luck attaining that, Space Cadet (unless you're reading this in the year 2056 in which case space travel will be like a family trip to Branson). You have to balance between pushing yourself to accomplish a challenging goal, but also making it realistic.

relevant
How does achieving this goal align with your priorities? If you say, "I want to be a millionaire by the time I'm 25," that's great, but how does that goal tie back into your priorities? If none of your priorities have anything to do with money or financial independence, then the goal is not relevant. Your goals must be relevant to your priorities.

time bound
What is your cut-off date for acheiving this goal? There should be a set finish line, so you are pushing yourself to achieve your goal. Without a timeline for accomplishing the goal, it is very easy to get off track, and you just get to it when you get to it. A goal without a deadline is just a wish.

write it down

Your goals must be written down. When you write down your goal, what you want to accomplish not only becomes clearer, it becomes a visual reminder of what you're trying to do. When you write it down, you are making a commitment with yourself. It's more than a wish that can change based on current circumstances.

make it happen

Now it's time to transfer those goals over into your schedule. Once you have established your goals, you need to create some specific steps in order to accomplish those goals. For example, if you want to raise $5,000 for charity at your next club fundraiser, that won't just happen on its own, right? You may need to create a checklist of things that need to happen. Your list may include calling local businesses for support, brainstorming ideas to raise money, talking with friends to get them involved, etc. You need to create a list of tasks that must get done in order to accomplish that bigger goal.

Now that you have a list of items and tasks that you need to be working on in order to accomplish your goal, you will want to actually schedule in your planner when you will do those tasks. When you create a schedule and a plan, you are taking time to save time. Block out realistic amounts of time to accomplish specific tasks and follow through with your game plan.

Throughout the entire process of creating and carrying out your goals, continue to do two things: constant evaluation and intense focus. Continually look at your schedule to make sure that your priorities are reflecting how you spend your time. If they're not and everything seems out of whack, make some changes so your schedule truly reflects your priorities. On top of all this, stay focused on your goals. Remember the bigger picture of why you're doing what you're doing.

chapter thirty-three
what do I want to do with my life?

Ah, the million dollar question. Has everyone and their dog been asking you that since you finished high school? If you don't know precisely what you want to do with your life, the question gets a little annoying when it's asked over and over and over.

Years ago when you were just a little tike, this was a fun question to kick around. Because everyday you could be something different. On Monday, you could be a firefighter. On Tuesday, you could be an Olympic athlete. On Wednesday, you could be an astronaut. On Thursday, you could be in a boy band. On Friday, you realized a boy band was not such a great idea after all. It was fun to day dream about these options as a kid, because it didn't matter back then. But now that you're on the verge of actually having to answer that question, you may be finding that it is not as easy to answer as you had hoped.

There are countless options of what you can do, but really nailing down the career path you want to start on can be a challenge. Let me provide you with a few broad principles to consider as you try to determine what you want to be when you grow up:

don't pick something for the money

It is far too common that people make career decisions based on where they think the money is. Life is too short to do something just for a nice paycheck. Generally, our generation agrees that we would rather make less and enjoy what we do than make more and hate life. But money talks, so it's easy to get pulled towards something with a bigger salary. In my opinion, if you do something well enough, people will pay you for it.

pick a career for you, not your family

Maybe in your family, there has been some type of "generational career" that several members of your family have done. Perhaps there is a family business that you are feeling pressured to be a part of. But just like those who follow the money, you need to find work that *you* are passionate about, not what your parents think you should do for a living. If there's a family business you want to be a part of, then great, but don't do something just because you feel you have to or because you're supposed to.

don't stress about what the "hot" industry may be

Every year there is a new "hot" industry that offers a ridiculous amount of hype by promising unlimited income potential, endless growth, countless opportunities, and blah, blah, blah. I'm sure they don't promote offering "blah," but that's what most of it is. If you spend your life trying to find the "hot" industry, you will be bouncing around for the rest of your life. Do you remember in the late 1990s when the "hot" thing was to have some type of e-commerce website? It became a modern day gold rush, but today most of the companies that were started during that time are no longer even in business.

consider how long your working life will be

For me, I felt a huge stress because I thought that whatever I decided to do after college would be what I would do for the rest of my life. But in reality, nothing could be further from the truth. Think about it. If you start your career at age 22 and work until you're 65 years old, that means you will work for 43+ years. How many adults do you know who have worked at the same job doing the same work for 43 years? Very few. The U.S. Department of Labor says that each generation will average more job moves and career changes than the previous generation.

So while those are certainly some solid principles to consider when looking at potential job opportunities, what are some criteria you should be looking for in a career? Here are my top three criteria:

passion

What are you passionate about? For some people, this is a very easy question to answer, but for others, it poses more of a challenge. This was a very difficult question for me, and it certainly took some time and soul searching to figure out. Today, I get paid to do what I love which involves speaking, writing, and make a difference in the lives of others. It is important that you don't confuse passion with enthusiasm. You can be a very mellow, introverted individual and still care passionately about something. Often times we think of passionate people as slightly crazy and overly energetic to the point that it makes you concerned for your safety. But rather, passion is about doing something you love and find meaningful and sharing that passion with the world.

talent

What are you good at? Let's be honest: people don't want to do something they suck at. I like playing sports, but if I'm competing against someone who is killing me, and I'm no good at the game, then it is no fun anymore. People want to do things they are good at. What is it in your world that has always come naturally to you? You don't have to spend massive amounts of time practicing or working at it. It is just something that you've always been able to do. Maybe it is something with athletics, music, art, problem solving, or even your compassion for others. If you have to work, wouldn't you rather do something you're good at? It'll make your job a heck of a lot easier.

enjoyment

What do you like to do? If you have to make a living doing something, wouldn't you rather do something that you enjoy? Unfortunately, though, so many people live their lives with the mentality of "Thank God, it's Friday" to "Oh God, it's Monday." I may be weird, but I actually love Monday mornings. Why? Because I get to do something I really enjoy. If you don't look forward to Mondays, something may need to change. Now don't get me wrong. Just because you are doing something you are passionate about, good at, and like to do, doesn't mean you will enjoy every minute of the day. With every job, regardless of how much you like it, there are elements that come with the territory that you may not enjoy.

Finding work that you are passionate about, good at, and that you like to do is one of the most important things you can do with your life right now. When you consider how much of your life you will spend doing some type of work, it just seems logical that you would take the time to find something you love.

chapter thirty-four
should I be networking?

Absolutely! College is a prime opportunity to begin to expand your network. Think of your network like a spider web. One that captures small insects and allows you to devour them for your own good. Okay, scratch that last part. But your network is like a web of people who you know and who know you. That network of people may lead to future jobs, business opportunities, relationships, new friendships, and other open doors you may not even realize yet. Because college is a launchpad for the rest of life, it's a great place to build on that network. Here are a few networking tips:

networking is more than facebook

When students think of networking, we generally think of "social network" as in Facebook, Twitter, or LinkedIn. And while each of those sites (and the 473 new social networking sites that have been created in the last 12 minutes) do serve a purpose and can contribute to our networking efforts, they can't be the sole source. If you built your entire people network on MySpace or Xanga, who would your network consist of today? Tom from MySpace. And that's it. It's important to connect with people online, but it's even more important to have a human connection with people. There's something significant about shaking someone's hand, looking in their eyes, sitting down for coffee together and being fully present with them, versus sending them a tweet or a Facebook message.

buy people lunch

We all need to eat. At least I do. I like food. Since most people will be eating at some point today, why not use it as an opportunity to connect with others. When I want to connect with someone I've never met, I generally ask if I can buy them lunch or coffee. It's a small investment of money on your part that may lead to something big. What's the worst that could happen? They could say "no." Ouch. That hurt. I'm sure you're emotionally scarred now. But the potential upside to that lunch or coffee meeting could be huge. I'm currently mentoring and managing an up-and-coming speaker who was interested in doing what I do. How did we first connect? He sent me an email and asked if he could buy me lunch. Yes please.

it's not all about you

If the whole point of meeting someone else and expanding your network is all about how people can best help you, that will quickly turn others off. When I meet new people, I like to ask about their life, hopes, and dreams. They may say something that triggers something in my own mind about how I could help them or someone I could connect them with. In the book *How To Win Friends And Influence People* by Dale Carnegie, he says, "You can make more friends in two months by becoming interested in other people than you can in two years by trying to get other people interested in you." Good stuff right there.

your age is one of your most valuable commodities

There's something about being young and ambitious that connects and resonates with most people. Most people remember when they were you're age trying to figure out the world for themselves, so they often are willing to help and support you. Take advantage of your youth to connect with people that may not take the time to meet with you if you were 10 years older.

connect with like-minded people

Part of your goal for connecting with people is for you to be able to help them or for them to be able to help you. That means it helps if you find like-minded people. If you are majoring in video game design, and you're joining the Future Heart Surgeons Of America club on campus, that probably won't do much for your network in the future. Find clubs, programs, and activities on campus where you can connect with people who have similar interests, goals, and future ambitions as you. At the same time, there's nothing wrong with getting outside your bubble from time to time. Don't limit yourself to just like-minded people, but have purpose behind how you build your network.

So who can you network with? Professors, the staff in the career guidance office, classmates who share your major, parents of friends, and members of various clubs and groups. Your network will become one of your most valuable resources long-term, so take advantage of the opportunity to begin building and expanding that network while in college.

chapter thirty-five
how do I make my resume stand out?

You absolutely need a resume. A resume is basically a marketing piece that you use to sell yourself as an employee to the companies and organizations that you are interested in working for. A resume is a quick snapshot of, not only your skills and abilities as an employee, but also the quality of person that you are. There are several elements that your resume needs to include:

contact information

Assuming they like you (which hopefully they will) and want to move forward in the interview process, it would probably be helpful for them if they had a way to contact you! Make sure you provide all the necessary information including your full name, mailing address, home phone, cell phone, and email address. They probably won't need your Facebook or Twitter info (although they may find it for themselves...more on that in a minute). Of course if you send them a friend request and they deny you, it's not looking good for you.

education history

I know you aced kindergarten, and second grade was the best three years of your life, but employers don't really care much about what you did in elementary or even in middle school. What they want to see is how you did in high school and college. Remember you're trying to stand out, so mention anything that sets you apart such as a good GPA or a high rank in class. You might leave out that your favorite subjects were lunch and recess.

work experience

Here you can include any type of work experience you've had including part-time jobs, volunteer work, or internships. Employers aren't looking for potential employees who just talk a big game about what they *could* do, but they want students who have the experience to back it up. If you haven't had many jobs in the past, you can still demonstrate your skills with other experiences including involvement in your local church, leadership in clubs, or businesses that you've been involved with (i.e. babysitting or mowing lawns). Simply look for ways to show how you've displayed high levels of responsibility.

applicable skills

Especially if you are applying for a technical job, include any type of skills you have such as knowledge of software programs, computer systems, office equipment, or programming and design skills. You might want to leave out some of your lesser known talents such as your nunchuck skills, your ability to sleep for days at a time, or your unhealthy fascination with fire.

relevant categories

Depending on what type of job you are applying for, you may want to consider adding another category to show any related awards, significant achievements, leadership roles you've held, or just a paragraph of why you're so awesome.

Once you have compiled all these elements into a resume format, here are a couple of other tips to remember when putting it all together:

think of yourself as a brand, not a piece of paper

A resume is simply a piece of paper detailing all of your awesomeness. And it would be nice if potential employers formed an opinion about you based solely on what was on that sheet of paper. But in today's world, that's not the case. It's more and more common for potential employers to Google you and look at your profiles on Facebook, Twitter, or YouTube. They want to see behind the curtain at who you really are. So maybe tagging yourself in the picture from that crazy party wasn't such a good idea after all.

You have to begin to think beyond a piece of paper. Think of yourself as a brand. We all know celebrities, athletes, and artists who have established themselves as a brand. Is your impression of them based solely on what their resume might say? Probably not. You've formulated your own impression of them on a variety of factors. Potential employers are doing the same thing with you. Sure your resume will contribute to your brand, but it's also about how you dress, how you conduct yourself in an interview, how prompt you are, and of course who you are on Facebook or Twitter. All those things will contribute to your brand. You're not just a piece of paper anymore.

one size doesn't fit all

Each job you apply for will be slightly different than the next. This makes it very difficult to have a one-stop resume that fits what everyone is looking for. Take the time to customize your resume to the job. If you apply for a web programming job, bulk up the section about your programming skills and experience. If you're applying for a less technical job, they may not care as much about your expertise in that area.

k.i.s.s. (keep it simple, stupid)

There is no need to write a small novel about your life, and how great you are. Keep it short, sweet, and to the point. Your resume really shouldn't be any longer than one or two pages. This is more than enough space to communicate the main points, and will help you cut out all the excess junk that an employer won't care about. Anything longer than two pages may never even get read by potential employers.

remember to proofread

You would think this would be common sense, wouldn't you?! And yet still, there are always resumes people submit to potential employers that have typos. If you're an employer, and you receive a resume that is littered with typos, does that make you want to hire that person? Ov kors nott! So take the time to do more than spell check; print it out, and go over it with a fine-tooth comb.

always include a cover letter

A cover letter is the perfect way to introduce yourself to the potential employer and be able to express your interest in the job. This will be the first thing they read from you, so keep in mind the old saying, "You never get a second chance to make a first impression." Take the time to write a clear and personalized cover letter that makes them intrigued by you, before they ever see your resume.

think outside the box

The bigger the company, the more resumes they receive. And they all look the same. Resumes tend to follow a basic formula, so think through what you could do to stand out from the crowd. What if in addition to a resume, you included a link to a website you created with a short video or pictures introducing yourself? What if the domain was your name? I own GrantBaldwin.com and have actually purchased the domain names for all my kids. Ideas like that will make you memorable in a sea of resumes. And no matter what your little sister says, a glitter-covered resume will not help you stand out.

Sometimes we think a resume is necessary only when we start applying for career positions. But a resume is necessary even now. It's a living, breathing document you should regularly be updating. Start your resume your freshmen year and keep up with it. Of course it's used in job interview scenarios, but it's also relevant with scholarships, internships, and leadership positions. If you wait till the last minute to put it together, it will show. Take the time to do it right, and do it with excellence.

chapter thirty-six
what should I ask in a job interview?

Well first of all, congratulations that you even got the interview. Hopefully that means your resume was halfway decent, as we discussed in the previous chapter!

Now that we're to the interview stage of the process, there are some simple things you can do to avoid completely making a fool of yourself. Wear deodorant. Don't say "yes, sir" or "no, sir" if you're being interviewed by a woman. Limit the cussing from that potty mouth of yours. Don't belch. You know, just the usual public manners stuff that your Mommy taught you. Here are some other tips to help you with your interview:

prepare, prepare, prepare

Think of a job interview like a final exam in school. If you cram for it the night before and drink a couple of cases of Red Bull to keep you going, you're probably going to be a disaster come test time. But if you take the time to study and prepare, you can go in feeling calm, cool, and collected. Plus, your eyes won't be twitching from the caffeine buzz.

So how do you prepare? Think through possible questions they might ask and how you will respond. Google the company and learn everything you can, not only about the organization, but also about the person interviewing you. Practice actually saying what you want to communicate in the interview. Review your resume, and know what points you want to highlight.

Basically, just be prepared. A potential employer knows if you are taking this opportunity seriously or if you're just wasting their time. And do I really have to remind you to be on time?! You should actually plan to be early. Don't risk issues such as traffic, parking problems, or just general time management issues.

dress the part

A survey of over 3,000 hiring managers by CareerBuilder.com found that more than half, 51%, said the biggest mistake a potential candidate can make during an interview is dressing inappropriately.[1] Leave the bling at home and lean more towards the conservative side. Wear clean and professional clothes, and don't overdo it with the accessories. This means you probably shouldn't wear that Superman t-shirt you got at the local thrift shop for a nickel. No cleavage, no navels, no butt cracks!

don't blame the past

In that same survey by CareerBuilder.com, they found that the second biggest mistake an applicant can make in an interview is talking negatively about a current or former employer. This communicates a bad attitude, and perhaps sends the message that you are difficult to work with. While you don't need to sugar-coat everything and say that every boss and every job you've had have been perfect, don't spend the entire interview railing on the past.

follow up

You may not realize it, but the interview doesn't end after you walk out the door. After the interview, always send a handwritten thank you card or letter. The interviewer didn't have to take the time to talk with you, so show your appreciation for their time but also reiterate your interest in the position. Also, take the time after an interview to evaluate how you did. It

---

[1] http://www.reuters.com/article/2008/03/13/us-jobs-interviews-idUSSP687020080313?pageNumber=2&virtualBrandChannel=0

probably won't be your last interview ever, so determine what went well and some areas for improvement for next time around.

be you

The biggest thing you have to do in an interview is be you. (Wow, that rhymed a lot.) An employer wants to meet the real you, not some imaginary person that you try to present yourself as. They want to hire an actual person, so you have to show them what they are getting. While you may try to present yourself as what you think they are looking for, in reality, they just want to get to know the real you. So be you in the interview. (I did it again.)

It's important to remember that a job interview isn't just about them quizzing you. It is also a chance for you to get to know them as a company. You may be totally pumped about a particular job, only to find out that the potential boss, who interviewed you, is a jerk.

Once you actually get into the interview itself, sometimes your nerves may get the best of you, and you think your only role is to answer their questions. While you, of course, want to put your best foot forward and try to make a solid impression, don't miss out on the opportunity to conduct an interview of them. Hopefully, you're not so mentally drained from their pop quiz that you don't ask any questions of your own.

By asking them some questions, you are also communicating your level of interest in the position. You are letting them know that you are not there to just go through the formality of the interview, but that you are genuinely interested in this opportunity. If I'm interviewing someone for my company, and they have zero questions, it communicates to me that they're really not that interested. Here are 10 good questions to toss out there:

if I do an outstanding job in my role, what would that look like?

This will help you define expectations a little better. Your understanding of "success" in the new role may be completely different than your boss'. Be clear up front about expectations, and always get it in writing before the job begins. It's also a good idea to ask the opposite question: "If I'm a complete disaster, what would that look like?"

what do you like best about working here?

The person interviewing you was once in the same position that you're in now. Obviously they've done something right and have been there for a decent length of time, so it would be interesting to hear their perspective on the company. Are they positive and upbeat about the organization, or do they spend a lot of time ripping the company?

what are you passionate about?

This question will help you learn a little more about your potential boss. While some people would advise against this type of question, the reality is that people want to work with people they like. Use discretion when asking this question, but it can help determine if you like your potential boss, and they determine if they like you.

what types of advancement and growth opportunities are available here?

If the job you are interviewing for offers no room for growth, you should take that into consideration. If you've already hit the glass ceiling before you even start, is that really a job you want? Determine what kind of opportunities there are for moving into management or other roles that interest you.

what is the average day / week like in my role?

This helps you get a good idea of what you'll actually be doing on a day-to-day basis. Are you working with others or by yourself? Is your job more people-oriented or task-oriented? You get the idea.

what is the company culture like?

You have to ask yourself if this is a place you really want to work at. If you're casual and laid back, but you notice everyone is in suits and ties, nobody smiles, and joking is not permitted, is that the type of culture you want to work in? But if you're very serious and professional, then their Slurpee machine in the break room, spontaneous Wiffle ball tournaments in the office, and attire of shorts and flip flops could be concerning to you.

what is your leadership style?

You should consider what kind of boss you want to work for. Does the boss seem to be more of a micromanager who is always in your business? Or do they come across as more hands off and allow you room to breathe, but perhaps may not provide much feedback or instruction?

is there anything I should ask you that I haven't already asked?

This is a great question. This will tell them that you're serious about the job, and it will also show how honest they are willing to be with you.

where do we go from here?

By asking this, I don't mean you're checking to see if they want to go grab a bite for lunch or if they have time to catch a movie. Do you have another interview with them or someone else? Do you have to fill out additional paperwork? Will they be contacting you once they've made the decision, either good or bad? You should get a clear idea of what the next steps will be.

can I contact you if I think of other questions?

A question like this keeps the door open for future communication with them. Again, it also reminds them that you are very interested in the opportunity. Don't take this as an invitation to stalk them, however. Most interviewers generally frown on stalkers.

I know if you're interviewing for a dream job that you are doing everything you can to put your best foot forward. But remember, the company is also trying to do the same. They want to hide their flaws and zits as much as you want to hide yours. So take advantage of the opportunity to ask them the difficult questions as well.

chapter thirty-seven
where can I find a great internship?

Ah, the challenge of the internship. It is one of those Catch 22s in life. In order to get a great job when you graduate, you have to have solid experience, but how do you get solid experience without having a good job in the first place? In order to solve this great mystery, let me introduce you to my good friend, and soon to be yours, *internship*.

An internship is a great opportunity for you to, not only gain valuable experience in an industry, but also to essentially test drive a career path to see if it is something you want to pursue. In addition to it being a good idea, it may also be a necessity. Most college degree programs require that you complete an internship prior to graduating.

Before you even begin to search for an internship opportunity, evaluate what you're looking for. If you don't know what you want in an internship, how will you ever know if you've found it? (That's deep, I know.) Figure out if you desire to gain some specific skills, work for a certain company, have a unique experience, or simply fulfill a college requirement. Once you've taken the time to answer the *why* part of the equation, then it is time to answer the *how*. Here are some resources to find that killer internship you're looking for:

school / career counselors

Sometimes I wonder if school counselors were once part of the CIA – they have contacts with everybody. Even the organizations and companies that you think are impossible to get hooked up with, your counselor knows a guy who knows a guy who can get you in. It's crazy, I know. Slightly creepy and yet equally awesome. Sit down with your college advisor and discuss what it is you're looking for and see where that takes you. Most colleges and universities also have a Career Center that should have plenty of resources to help you out.

your network

When I say "your network," I'm talking about all the connections you have with people, from friends to family to teachers to that strange guy you met on the Internet. When you talk with other people in your network about opportunities you're looking for, you'll be amazed at what you find. Maybe you have a friend who is in a similar internship that you're interested in who might be able to get you in. Maybe a relative or a family friend works at an organization that sounds appealing. All around you are opportunities for incredible internships, but you have to let your network know what you're after.

This is where getting involved on your campus in order to expand your network can really be beneficial long-term. If you just sit in your dorm all day and avoid human interaction and sunlight, first of all, you're going to have really pasty skin. Second, you miss out on opportunities to join clubs, groups, a fraternity or sorority, or other organizations that will help you to meet new people and expand your network.

the power of the web

In the digital age that we live, an effective, but often overlooked method for finding internships, is utilizing the power of the Internet. Go online and search, not just "internships," but specifically a description of what you're looking for or companies that fit your criteria. A lot of companies that have a strong presence online will have links within their website to internship opportunities. If you can't find a specific page, it never hurts to contact someone within the company who seems like the closest fit to what you're looking for.

Once you have a list of several internship possibilities that seem attractive, go back through the process like you did when deciding on a college. Compare the pros and cons of each option, and see where you land.

chapter thirty-eight
I'm interested in a unique career... how do I get started?

More and more today, students are pursuing careers that are a little unique and non-traditional. Our parents were limited to the normal options of doctor, teacher, accountant, lawyer, farmer, etc. But today, we have options like Apple app developer, YouTube personality, blogger, or motivational speaker. Where do you go to school for those careers? What kind of major has any remote alignment with something so unique?

I read an article about a guy who was a corporate lawyer in New York City making over $100,000 a year. He was good at what he did but didn't necessarily enjoy it. His true passion was...(wait for it)...playing with Legos. Eventually, this guy fulfills his dream and quits the lawyer job to play with Legos. Professionally. Wow.

If you've ever been to a Lego Store or LegoLand, you've seen some of the massive structures built out of Legos. That's this guy's job! But as passionate as he may be about playing with Legos and building amazing structures, I don't know of any college that offers a degree in "Professional Lego Playing." (If your school does, please email me!)

So what do you do you when you're interested in a unique or different career that doesn't fall in line with the traditional workforce?

don't reinvent the wheel

Find mentors. One of the best things you can do is learn from others. When I started this business as a speaker, I thought I was a fairly decent communicator, but I didn't know much about the speaking business. So I spent, and still do, a lot of time networking with other speakers who are successful. Find people who you respect and admire and learn from them. There is no need to reinvent the wheel.

If you want to be successful, one of the best things you can do is find successful people and learn what they did to become successful. A great advantage you have is you are young and are hungry to learn. Successful people have been in your shoes before, so they are often much more likely to help out. Take people to lunch. Ask lots of questions. Take lots of notes. And learn everything you can.

When you contact people, ask them something specific that is simple for them to answer to get the conversation started. I get emails from people interested in being speakers (which I enjoy helping out), but when people ask "how do I become a speaker?," it's like asking a doctor, "how do you do surgery?" or asking a builder, "how do you build a house?" That's not an easy question to answer with a simple email response. Try something like simpler and more specific.

read like crazy

More than ever before, books, blogs, YouTube videos, and magazines are being created for very niche industries and markets. Take whatever topic or career you're interested in, and Google it to see what I mean. You're bound to find other people interested in the same subject matter. You're also likely to find people doing exactly what you want to do. When you do find them (and you will), don't stalk them, but reach out to them like we just talked about.

When we find people doing something similar to what we want to do, it's easy to get fixated on where they're at today. It's easy to see someone's success and be consumed by the destination that we forget to learn about the journey. People work years and years to become an overnight success, so learn *how* they got to where they're at. I love reading biographies of people who have been successful in business, because you get to see the steps they took to get where they're at. Reading about the founders of Facebook, Apple, Amazon or Google and where they're at today is intimidating, but it brings a little confidence when you learn that at one point, they were just individuals with an idea and a dream.

start something

One of the best ways to learn about your unique career idea is to just start doing it. If you want to be a speaker, start looking for opportunities to speak. If you want to be a professional Lego builder, start building your own unique structures and post pictures on Facebook or a blog. Whatever it is you want to do, start doing it.

You don't need to wait until you have it all figured it out and know exactly the route you'll take to achieving your dream. Your first step doesn't have to be anything huge or amazing. It may just be some simple little hobby you start on the side so you can learn more about that business or industry. The Roman philosopher Seneca said, "Luck is when preparation meets opportunity." You're not going to stumble into that amazing dream career opportunity unless you do a little prep work of your own.

It's also important to realize just because you're interested in a unique career doesn't mean that college is no longer relevant for you. There are plenty of more "generic" majors that can give you knowledge and education to apply to your unique career endeavor. Majors like Communications, Media, or General Business are all applicable to most careers.

In today's world, you don't have to settle for a traditional, 9-5 office gig. There are countless opportunities that don't follow the normal path. If you're legitimately interested in something different, do the work necessary to learn about that career, and then bust your butt to make it happen.

chapter thirty-nine
should I start a business?

Being your own boss, calling the shots, building an empire as an entrepreneur sounds really cool. We're all familiar with the college student success stories of those who started and built incredible businesses like Facebook (Mark Zuckerberg), Dell (Michael Dell), Microsoft (Bill Gates), and Google (Sergey Brin and Larry Page). Being an entrepreneur and starting your own business is one of the most exciting career paths you can take. And while the potential rewards and benefits are limitless, there are an equal number of risks to consider. Here are some things to think about before starting a business:

the entrepreneur

A lot of times, we get caught up with the *idea* of having our own gig and running our own business, but just thinking about it and actually living in it on a daily basis are very different things. Before we get too deep into talking about the *how* of starting a business, you have to answer some other self-evaluating questions first:

why do you want to start your own business?
Do more than just respond with a surface answer, but take the time to really evaluate the *why?* If you have no sense of why you're doing something, it will get very frustrating to you very quickly. Just having a business for the sake of having a business is not that appealing.

how would you measure the success of your business?
This also ties back into the *why* question. Obviously a major part of measuring success in a business is profit. If you're not making a profit or you're losing money, then you have a hobby not a business. So beyond the financial and profit side of running a business, how would you measure the success of what you do? If it's just money, that will get old very quickly.

what characteristics do you have that would make you a good entrepreneur?
Don't get me wrong, being an entrepreneur is phenomenal and can be extremely rewarding, but it is also very difficult. You've got to be immensely passionate about what you're doing, or it will get real old real fast. You've got to be determined but have the wisdom to know the difference between stubbornness and stupidity. You've got to be disciplined to get the work done even when no one is telling you to.

the idea

You're probably in one of two places right now. Either you have an idea, and you just need to figure out how to make it happen, or you are interested in being an entrepreneur, but you're not really sure what kind of idea you would like to pursue. You want to find an idea that fits these three criteria:

something you love
What are you deeply passionate about? What are the things that really get you fired up? How can those passions and loves translate into a business idea?

something you know (or will learn about)
If you're going to be working in a particular industry, you need to know what you're talking about.

something that gives you what you're looking for
Would you rather offer a product or a service? Would you rather work from home by yourself or have an entire team of employees? Is this a long-term business idea or just a side project? Know from the beginning what you're looking for with this business idea.

Once you have the idea down, one of the biggest challenges is just getting started. With so many things to do, where do I even begin? Start small. Don't try to build a massive operation overnight. Don't quit your day job to pursue this dream. Build slow.

the money

Starting a business is great, but of course it does cost money. Everything about running a business costs money, but it doesn't have to be expensive. When you're a college student, it can feel like it is difficult to have the cash necessary to start something. Let me give you a couple of principles to help on the financial side of starting a business:

start small
You don't have to build this empire to the size of Apple or Google overnight. Start small right where you are at. That means if you are wanting to start a business mowing lawns, it probably wouldn't be the smartest idea to go buy $20,000 of equipment on a credit card, take out a huge ad in the Yellow pages (is that even still in existence?), buy billboards and TV ads, and just sit and wait. Just start small. Start with five yards and do a killer job on those five. Then build it from there. Whenever you start small, you get the chance to slow down and learn the business a little more. The more you get into it, you may realize that particular business isn't for you.

build it over time
It is easy to want to get in a rush and try to have this huge empire overnight. But it just doesn't work like that. It takes time for things to develop so we have to change our mentality from a microwave to a crock pot. Things in crock pots take time, but they are sure good when they come out. We want the business to be a full-time job, or we want it to be successful as soon as possible, but if you end up rushing the process, you may cause yourself and the business more damage than it's worth. Avoid biting off more than you can chew.

don't borrow money
You should have figured this out by now if you read the money chapters! I say this, because I've been on both sides of the coin. My wife and I used to have an eBay business and made virtually all our purchases on a credit card. That was a great way to rack up a lot of unnecessary debt. When I started this business as a speaker, we've bootstrapped it the entire time

and have never borrowed money. We pay cash, or we don't get it. It's a lot less stressful that way.

Being an entrepreneur is one of the most exciting and challenging things you can do with your life. I work extremely hard at what I do and while there are certainly plenty of risks associated with having your own business, I wouldn't trade it for an office job any day.

chapter forty
how do I find a place to live?

Living on your own is one of the most exciting parts of growing up. For years, you've lived with Mom and Dad, and now you're ready to spread your wings and leave the nest. The challenge is now you have to find another nest to live in. Living on your own can seem really appealing, but once you actually get out on your own, it is also easy to realize how good you had it living with your parents. (You probably never imagined you would have that thought!) Let's explore some options, and the pros and cons of each:

live in the dorms

If you're taking a full load of classes in college, living on campus in the dorms is a great option for you. If you're living in the dorms, you are probably within walking distance of everywhere you would need to be, depending on the size of the campus.

This obviously saves you money on gas. Of course if you're not a very social person, and you like to go to bed at 9:30pm each night, dorm life may not be a good fit for you. Also, determine how much you will actually utilize the meal plan that may come with living in the dorms. It's always a good idea to do the math for what the room and board fee is, and figure out what it actually costs to live in the dorms on a monthly basis. Compare this to your other options from a financial standpoint.

rent an apartment / house

Renting either an apartment or a house fairly close to campus is a very common option for college students. If you're a campus socialite, living off campus may give you the feeling of being disconnected from everything, however, you will definitely have more peace and quiet than what the dorm offers. Plus you will likely have more space than your average dorm room. Of course, you have a new level of financial responsibility when renting. While some rentals offer an all-inclusive monthly cost, most require that you pay certain utilities such as electric, water, internet, or cable which can get expensive. In addition, you have to pay your rent to your landlord every month, so you better have the money when rent is due. One upside to a rental is that you are usually not responsible for routine repair and maintenance expenses.

A great way to help offset some of this expense is to share it with a roommate. If you do end up with a roommate, make sure it is someone you trust and enjoy being around (they will be there a lot!). Also, make sure you establish up front some ground rules and what your agreement will be on certain issues. For example, who pays for groceries? Will you split all monthly expenses 50/50? What happens if you need to go to bed, but they want to have friends over? Once you establish this agreement, make sure you put it in writing, have both of you sign it, and keep that document filed away. On a side note, it's important to realize that your best friend may make a horrible roommate. Even if you're moving in with a close friend, have a contract and get it in writing.

buy a house

Although this may seem like the most appealing option, it has the most risks for students. The common assumption is that if you are living in an apartment and paying rent, you are throwing money away. But if you buy a house, you know your monthly payment is actually going towards something. While this sounds nice in theory, there are so many more risks associated with owning a house that it can become a curse instead of a blessing. When you own a house, you are responsible for everything. If the water heater goes out, you're fixing it. If the roof has a leak, you're paying for it. If anything goes wrong, it falls back on you. Plus you have the added expense of homeowners insurance and property taxes. Having said all of that, here are a couple of criteria to have in place before buying a house.

- Be Debt Free – You don't need other payments and bills to add to the burden of owning a home.

- Have An Emergency Fund – This is that rainy day fund for the repairs and upkeep expenses you will have.

- Put As Much Down As Possible – The more you put as a down payment on the house, the less risk you have for yourself. Shoot for 10%-20% and avoid zero-down offers.

- Get a Fixed Interest Rate – You should avoid getting a mortgage with a variable interest rate. These can fluctuate too much and backfire on you.

stay at home

The least appealing, but perhaps the most practical option for housing, is just staying put with your folks. I know this sounds as exciting as watching grass grow, but it may very well be worth it. If they live even remotely close to where you will be going to school, your added gas expense is more than offset by little to no living expenses. Don't just assume you have a free ride, but any contribution you make to the living expenses of staying at home will be far less than living on your own. Is it the most attractive option? Maybe not. Is it the most sensible? Probably.

So where do you go from here? There are several factors to consider when finding a place to live:

proximity

Take into consideration how close your place will be to everywhere else you live life, including school, your job, your friends' places, and of course, the nearest Walmart. If you have really low rent, but you have to drive 45 minutes to get anywhere you need to go, is it worth it?!

finances

When looking for a place to live, you don't want to bite off more than you can chew financially. As you consider the financial side of the equation, think through the worst-case scenarios. If you have a roommate and they decide to move out, can you still afford the place on your own? Once you move in, what do you need to buy in order to make the place livable? As an example, our family is getting ready to move into a new house. The house was just renovated, so you would think it would be good to go. But there were no blinds in the entire house, so we had to drop an extra $900 on blinds for all the windows. Think these things through.

stage of life

Consider how permanent you want this place to be based on where you're at in life. If you are planning a major move in the next year, you probably don't want to be locked into a lengthy lease or anything remotely permanent. Think through possible job relocations, family, relationships or other situations that may cause you to move relatively soon.

area of town

In every city, there are areas of town where you would feel comfortable leaving your front door open at night. There are other places where you couldn't pay someone to live in. Consider not only how safe and secure you will feel in an area, but also how much peace and quiet you'll get.

Who you are is more important than what you do.

section five

life skills

chapter forty-one
who am I?

Since the beginning of time, people have struggled to find their identity and answer the question, "Who am I?" You would think it would be easier to figure out, but perhaps it is simply part of the journey of life. Human beings will go to great lengths to answer this question. People read books, seek psychics, solicit input, and take trips to find themselves.

Yet we continue to live with this ongoing identity crisis. Often times we live life as if we are part of a masquerade. We wear masks to disguise and cover who we really are for fear of what someone would think about us. We worry that if people know who we really are, they wouldn't like us or would think less of us. We end up trying to find our identities in other people, places, and things only to be left feeling empty inside. The journey to finding our identity and answering the question, "Who am I?" is a continual part of life.

For many, this journey really seems to gain intensity during college. This is one of the first times you're out on your own, you're determining what you want to do with your life, and the pressure of it can become quite powerful. It all becomes very real. Who am I and where is my life going? Here are some ideas to consider as you take this journey:

if you don't determine your identity, others will determine it for you

In our culture, it is easy to get sucked into the trap of letting others determine your identity for you. You know as well as I do that this is a major challenge in school because of the labels and stereotypes that get attached to people. Peer pressure is a real battle, and it is very easy to conform and go with the crowd. But until you begin to stand up for yourself, choose what you will and won't do, who you are and who you're not, people will walk all over you. If you allow that to happen, then you will have allowed other people to determine your identity for you. Standing up for yourself and determining your identity comes with consequences, both positive and negative. When you determine your identity and who you are as a person, you will probably lose friends, status or popularity. But when you establish who you are as a person, you will have more confidence and a stronger sense of self-worth.

your identity is not determined by people or stuff

It is extremely easy to attempt to find our identity in a relationship, a group of people, or possessions. But none of these items determine your value. Maybe you've seen this happen before: after a breakup of a relationship, some guys and girls are not even sure how to function independently of the other person because so much of their identity was wrapped up in that relationship. Or some people are consumed with their appearance and always think they are too fat, too skinny, too tall, or too short. They are obsessed with their looks or having the right clothes, and their entire identity as a person gets consumed by something superficial. How many people do you know whose entire identity is built upon their work and their career? Who you are is more important than what you do. Your identity is not found in a relationship, what you drive, where you live, what your grades are, the clothes you wear, your major, how you look, the way you talk, or who your friends are. Period.

ask those closest to you

Talk with those people in your life who love you the most, and ask them how they see you as a person. With this in mind, let me again stress the previous point that your identity is not found in what other people think of you. Often times we look at this in a negative connotation, but it can also be extremely positive when you talk with the people in your life who love you for you. These are people such as your parents, siblings, close friends, teachers, or others in your life that genuinely know and care about you. Ask them how they see you. Often times they have the ability to see what you don't, and they can tend to see the potential in yourself that you may overlook.

answer the question: who am I *not*?

A great way to begin to determine your identity and answer the question, "Who am I?" is to ask the opposite question: Who am I *not?* This is generally a simpler question to answer, because it is easier to identify those things that don't represent who we are. Use a question like this as a springboard to then be able to answer the original question, "Who am I?"

Quite honestly, I don't know if it's possible to ever arrive at a complete and solid answer to this question. We are living, breathing organisms, and who we are as individuals is continually evolving, changing, and growing. While that may be the case, continue to strive to answer this question. Your life will continue to change, but do the hard work to discover the core and foundation of who you are as a person. Doing so will bring enormous focus and clarity to your life.

chapter forty-two
how do I learn to live on my own?

Do you remember your first day of kindergarten? You had this feeling that was a mix of "This is going to be awesome," and "I hope I don't pee my pants!" You probably had the same emotional roller coaster your first day of middle school, and maybe even high school. You had that feeling when you got your driver's license, too, didn't you? Perhaps when you went on your first date or went to prom. I remember experiencing that wave of emotion during all of those moments of life, not to mention when I got married and became a father.

Each time we open a new chapter in the stories of our lives, it becomes very difficult to know what is next. It seems like just yesterday you started high school, and now here you find yourself entering the world of college. And before you know it, you'll be graduating and headed off to start your career in the real world.

If I had to make a guess, I'd bet the past few years could probably be described as comfortable for you. Why? Because you know how everything works. You know what you can and can't get away with in class. You've established a solid foundation of friends that you probably spend most of your time with. And for the most part, you think you've got life pretty much figured out up to this point.

But when you make that transition from high school to college and the real world, suddenly you are entering into the land of the unknown. The first day you went to kindergarten, you were excited for this new adventure, but you were terrified because you weren't entirely sure what you were supposed to be doing. You may have that same feeling now. You're completely excited that you're growing up, becoming an adult, and will soon experience more freedom than you've ever had. But inside, there's a freaked-out little kid who wants to sit in the corner, rock back and forth, suck his thumb, and be held by Mommy. (That's a pretty picture, isn't it?)

Let's be honest. It is easier to stay in a situation that you are comfortable in than to venture out into the unknown. It's easier to stay on the shore as opposed to jumping in the ocean. There is a fear that you don't know what's in the ocean or if you'll be able to swim. But if you always stay on the shore, you'll never experience the feeling of playing in the ocean. Besides, if you get freaked out, you can always pee in the ocean. Nobody will know the difference.

The point is this: on the first day of anything, you're freaked out and are probably sensing a minor anxiety attack. But after a while, you kind of figure things out, don't you? Over the first few weeks, you got the hang of kindergarten, and it wasn't too bad. One of my first weeks, I learned that you're not supposed to pull someone's chair out from underneath them. Prior to kindergarten, supposedly I didn't know that. I learned this is frowned upon. You figured out the game in high school, too, and thankfully you managed to navigate your way through. College and the real world are exactly the same way. At first, you're scared out of your mind, but over time you'll figure it out.

This happens long after high school and college. When my wife and I had our first daughter, we didn't know what the heck we were doing. We were shocked that the hospital just lets you come in, have a baby, and then sends you home with no instruction manual for what to do next! Let's be honest…there are plenty of people leaving hospitals with new born babies, and they are not ready to be parents. But they figure it out. They get into a rhythm and establish some habits of what it means to be parents.

It is all just part of the journey of growing up. While it may seem simpler and more convenient to sit on the shore for the rest of your life, that's no way to live. It's fine to be a little nervous about the future, but don't pee your pants over it (unless you're in the ocean). Eventually you'll figure it out, and get the hang of things. It's all part of the experience of growing up and becoming an adult. It's kind of like a reality check, isn't it? (That would make a great book title.)

chapter forty-three
how do I better manage my time?

Time management is about making a series of small, proactive choices to determine how to get the most out of your day. In high school and when you were living at home, your parents and the school system generally managed your time for you. You knew when you needed to be where. For the most part, you didn't have to worry too much about managing your time.

That's all changing. Entering into the land of college brings an enormous freedom to your schedule. Neither Mom nor Dad nor your teacher nor school counselor are telling you to get up for class, to start prepping for that exam, or to finish that reading assignment. They're not there to remind you not to stay up all night or sleep in through all your classes. It all falls on you. For some, that's exciting. For others, you just peed a little.

The dangerous thing is if you don't get a grasp on managing your time right now, it will be too late before you realize the consequences have already arrived. It's very easy to get caught up in the here and now. Why think about and plan for tomorrow when today is here? In high school, your assignments would generally come to you on a week-by-week basis. That meant it was rare that you needed to think and plan beyond this week. It's different in college. Not only do you need to think beyond today, but you really need the ability to see the entire semester. Often times in your first class, you'll get the syllabus that outlines the work that needs to be completed for the entire semester. You may have a 600-page reading assignment that isn't due for three months, but if you wait three months to get started on it, you're screwed.

You've heard the expression, "How do you eat an elephant? One bite at a time." The idea of eating an elephant seems daunting (and also probably illegal), so you have to divide the task into smaller bites. Rather than focusing on the entire elephant, just focus on the next bite. Here's how you could do that this semester:

1. The first step is to start with the big picture and look at your entire year or semester. Take all of your syllabi, and create a master list of all your major assignments, and order them by when they are due during the semester.

2. Take all of your big projects and assignments and create a simple timeline for what you need to have done at what points during the semester. As an example, if you have a 600-page English reading assignment due in 12 weeks, you know you need to read 50 pages each week to stay on track. If you have a 20-page Biology research paper due in six weeks, you know there will be a series of steps and tasks involved with that process. Your broken-down tasks may include deciding on a topic, creating an outline, spending 10 hours researching the subject, and writing a rough draft. Break the bigger assignment into smaller tasks.

3. At the beginning of each week (Sunday afternoon or evening works well), sit down and map out the 5-7 assignment tasks that need to get done in order to stay on track for that week. For this week, you may have read pages 100-150 for your English assignment. You also need to finalize your outline for that 20-page Biology paper. Don't worry about the entire semester. Just focus on this week.

Personally, I use an 80/20 system of planning my week. The 80/20 rule says that 20% of your efforts will give you 80% of your results. In most businesses, 20% of their products or services produce 80% of their revenue. In group projects, 20% of the people do 80% of the work. So if this is true (and it seems to be), you need to know what your 20% is for the week. So I make two columns. A 20% column and an 80% column. All of the most important tasks for that week go in my 20% column. Everything else that needs to get done goes into the 80% column.

4. Once you've established the big picture of the semester, and decided what you need to get done this week, then you can focus on today. For today, you don't have to read all 50 pages of your English assignment. You may only need to read 10 pages. Maybe your Biology paper outline falls under your 20% column, so you have down to complete that on Monday.

It takes a little planning up front to map out your semester, but it will save you enormous amounts of time. It's the same reason you plan the route you take before you head out on a road trip. You don't just start driving and every 100 miles look at a map and see if you're on track. Most students read a syllabus the first day and never look at it again until the professor reminds them three months into the semester that the project that is worth 50% of their grade is due on Thursday.

Stop being reactive with your time and start being proactive. Know where your time is going to go instead of wondering where it went. When you plan out your semester like this, you'll be much less stressed. It's no fun living every day feeling like you're forgetting something. You feel like you're missing something or you're supposed to be somewhere right now, but you're not really sure.

Planning also gives you an incredible amount of freedom. During the summer, I spend most afternoons at the pool with my wife and daughters. Is there more work that could be getting done? Sure. But since I've mapped out my year, when I complete what I need to get done for today, then I don't have to stress about if I have the time to go to the pool or go out with friends or sleep in. I know what comes next, because I've planned it that way. Now my job is to just work the plan.

chapter forty-four
how do I deal with stress?

Learning to deal and cope with stress is a skill that is necessary throughout life, but especially in college. As we've established, your move into college and the real world is one of the biggest transitions you'll have in life. You'll be taking college classes, beginning to crystallize a career path, possibly working part-time, joining clubs and social groups, building new friendships and relationships, and overall establishing life on your own. That's a lot of change, and generally change equals stress. You feel less stress when you're more adapted to a situation, but with so much newness and transition taking place, you're bound to be a little on edge.

A recent survey found that four out of ten college students report they feel stressed often. One out of five say they feel stressed most of the time. One out of four students experienced daily stress and one in ten had thoughts of suicide.[1] Not only does that tell us a lot of students feel stressed out, but that stress can lead to other serious issues including depression, eating disorders, and suicidal thoughts. Here are some steps for better managing and dealing with stress:

---

[1] http://stress.lovetoknow.com/Statistics_on_College_Student_Stress

identify the source

You can't fix something that you can't identify. Step back and really examine why you feel stressed. Do you feel an overwhelming pressure to do well in school? Are you taking too many classes? Are you having difficulties with friends, a relationship, or your roommate? Do you feel homesick, or is there something happening back home with your parents or family that is causing stress? Are you dealing with an overwhelming sense of peer pressure or something related to social acceptance?

Really think through and determine the cause of your stress. It's also important to identify whether this is just a temporary, stressful season or if this is more of a long-term feeling you've been having. For example, if finals week is coming up, you probably feel a little more frazzled and stressed about it all. Once you complete that last final, you should probably return to feeling normal again. But if after that final, you still feel stressed, that's a problem.

make necessary changes

It's meaningless to identify the causes of your stress if you're not going to do anything to fix the situation. What changes do you need to make to keep this from happening on a regular basis? Do you need to drop a class? Do you need to go home this weekend to be with family during a crisis? In addition to making changes to directly affect the stress causing issue, there's also basic, health-related habits you can do that will lower your stress level.

Simple things like making sure to get enough sleep. Eating properly and exercising from time to time. Even if you just go for a walk each day, it will make a huge difference. But if you continue doing what you've been doing, you're going to continue getting what you've been getting: stress. Make some changes today.

seek outside help and support

Start by talking with a trusted friend or confidant. This may be difficult for you. So many of us don't like to share our problems, stress, or insecurities with others. We don't want to bother someone else with our problems or appear weak, so we keep it all locked up. Here's a simple principle, though:

if you don't let it out, it stays in. Groundbreaking, I know. Think about it, though. What you don't let out and share with someone continues to bottle up and compound with all the other crap you have swimming inside you. We've all had deep conversations with friends or loved ones and come away feeling relieved or like a weight has been lifted. That's a great feeling of freedom. So don't keep all your stress bottled up. It will just make things worse.

Sometimes stress goes beyond what a simple conversation with a friend can help with. Every college campus has a counseling center and support staff to help students through difficult phases of life. Whether you just feel a small amount of stress or just feel completely overwhelmed, there's nothing wrong with talking to a professional who can help. It doesn't make you weak or a bad person. Admitting you need help or guidance is actually a sign of strength not weakness.

This major transition into college and life on your own can be extremely stressful. Take a step back and identify where that stress is coming from and then do what's necessary to better manage and cope with it.

chapter forty-five
how can I learn to make better choices?

Life is a series of choices. Everyday you are making literally hundreds of different choices. Sure there are plenty of choices that are inconsequential and generally meaningless. But there are also many choices that are seemingly small but can have a huge impact. What you eat for breakfast, what time you go to bed, whether or not you go to that party, who you hang out with, and whether or not you keep up on your homework may seem like small decisions, but they can have a huge impact on your life. Here's an example.

Did you realize that by eating 125 less calories each day, you could lose as much as 33 pounds over the next 31 months?! Did you realize that if you eat an extra 125 calories each day, you could gain 33 pounds in 31 months?![1] Think about how small and inconsequential 125 calories really is. We're talking about a few extra potato chips, a scoop of ice cream, half of a can of Coke, or a granola bar. It's not much. But that small choice can either leave a significant positive or negative effect.

---

[1] *The Compound Effect* by Darren Hardy

That same principle applies to most choices you make throughout the day. Not studying that extra 15 minutes may not seem like a big deal, but it can add up. You may think no one even notices if you skip a few classes here and there, but it matters. Why? Think all the way back to early elementary. You learned a basic life principle. Cause and effect. Every choice has a consequence. If we don't like the potential consequences, then we just need to altar the decisions we're making.

If you study and keep up on your school work, you are rewarded with good grades and potentially more opportunities. If you drink and break the law, you suffer from negative consequences. It's really pretty simple when you think about it. Here's the challenge though. Up until this point in life, you've been able to make a lot of your own decisions, but there were boundaries you had to stay within. As a senior in high school, Mom and Dad may have let you have a lot of freedom, but you still lived under their roof and had to play by their rules. You may have had the freedom to run around the yard, but there was still a fence keeping you in.

But once you arrive at college and you're out on your own, there really isn't a fence anymore. Sure you've still got rules and laws you have to follow and obey, but Mom and Dad aren't there telling you to quit playing video games and start studying. No one is telling you that you can or can't eat ice cream for breakfast. You don't have to get someone's permission to go to that Greek party. The boundaries are gone. All the decisions and choices are on you now.

No pressure. Don't screw it up.

Here's another key point to remember: your decisions determine your destination. Chew on that for a second. It's delicious. Go back and have seconds. Like we've said, every day we are making decisions, and we must remember that those decisions are leading somewhere. If you don't like where your life is headed, change your destination by changing your decisions. If I'm in Chicago and I want to go to Los Angeles, but I start driving east, I can have all the best intentions, hopes, and dreams in life to go to Los Angeles, but it doesn't matter, because my decisions are taking me to a different destination. When it comes to your grades, you are making decisions that are leading to a destination. When it comes to the people you hang out with, you are making decisions that are leading to a destination. When it comes to what you do with your money, you are making decisions that are leading to a destination.

Being a success in life or a complete failure doesn't come down to one single decision or choice. It's a collection of hundreds and thousands of decisions that led to where you are. People don't become alcoholics, get divorced or file bankruptcy as a single, stand alone decision. People don't become wealthy, have successful marriages and families, and have a healthy lifestyle because of a single decision. Every decision has a consequence. Take an extra moment to think about the ones you're making today.

chapter forty-six
how do I develop better communication skills?

In a technology-driven world where so many of us find ourselves staring at a screen throughout much of the day (phone, computer, TV, iPad, etc.), our communication skills tend to start slacking. Regardless of what career path you take, you're always going to be interacting with and dealing with people. Often times we focus so much on the technical skills of our future career that we miss the people skills that need improving.

Having good communication skills is more than being able to fire off an email, send a Facebook message, or rattle off a text. Although all those should be a part of your communication toolbox, they're not the only skills you need. It's critical you learn to develop solid face-to-face interaction and communication skills with other human beings. This includes communicating with roommates, professors, advisors, peers, and employers. I get it that it's much easier to send off an email to someone than it is to meet with them. But solid human communication skills take practice. When you meet with someone face-to-face, it builds a relationship more than what an email can do for you.

For some people, meeting face-to-face with others is no big deal. You feel comfortable and confident, and it doesn't bother you. For others, you may be petrified at the idea of having to meet with someone in person. But you'll never overcome that fear and self-doubt unless you actually get some practice. Stop hiding behind a screen and start meeting with people! They won't bite. Most people are very friendly and helpful. But you'll never know that unless you step out of your comfort zone.

Here's your homework assignment (as if you don't have enough already): Carry on a five minute face-to-face conversation with someone. It can't be a roommate or close peer. It can be an acquittance, a co-worker, a professor, or someone you'd like to get to know better (guys, please don't use this as an opportunity to hit on girls!). During those five minutes (which may feel like an eternity), ask lots of questions about them. Show more interest in their life, and be able to carry the conversation. Maintain eye contact (not in a stalker, creepy way though) and be engaged in what the other person has to say. This is how you get better at communicating. Practice. Just don't tell the other person they're your guinea pig.

Of course, being able to communicate in person is only part of the equation. Communicating also includes all the technology you know and love. Communicating effectively and efficiently includes being able to leave a voicemail, send a clear and concise email, and write with correct punctuation, grammar, and spelling. Here are some quick tips for communicating using technology:

have a purpose

Have you ever received a lengthy email telling you about something, but you're not really clear if the sender is wanting something back from you? Are you supposed to respond? Do you need to acknowledge you read it? What was the purpose in them sending you that email? Don't be that guy. Don't leave people guessing why you sent that email. Use a subject line that gives a clear summary of the email and then make it really clear why you're emailing them and if you need or expect some type of response or feedback.

check before sending

I can't tell you how many emails and Facebook messages I've received from students that are littered with spelling errors, grammar issues, and punctuation flaws. Go back to the basics. Use paragraphs and spacing. Spellcheck is nice, but it doesn't catch when you confuse there, they're, and their. Reread your email or text before hitting send. And don't use abbreviations.

don't waste words (or time)

It's easy to write an email or leave a voicemail and start rambling on and on and on and on. Don't do that. Get to the point. Don't beat around the bush. Offer some simple greeting or pleasantry, but don't spend the next four paragraphs talking about how your cat won a blue ribbon in some show over the weekend.

written words don't show emotion

I think we've all been guilty of reading someone's email or text and completely misinterpreting how it was meant to be read. That's not fun to be on either side of that equation. I've been on both, and it sucks. Studies show as much as 80% of communication comes through non-verbals (gestures, facial expressions, appearance, etc.). If you're sending an email that could be misconstrued or taken out of context, it's probably better to make a phone call. If you have an angry email you're getting ready to shoot off, I'd recommend waiting 24 hours and then re-read it before hitting send. You may also have a friend read your email to make sure it sounds the way you intend it to be read.

Communication skills are a huge part of being successful in business and in life. Don't hide behind a screen and consider that communication. Technology is part of communication, but in order to improve your communication/people skills, you need to also actually meet with people. That's kind of an important ingredient.

chapter forty-seven
how do I deal with difficult people?

Let's go ahead and put this out there. No one is as smart as you. Or as talented as you. Or understands you. Or is as nice as you. Or is as competent as you. Or as…well…you get the idea. Basically the world is full of a bunch of idiots except for you. And some days me. But that's about it. Everyone else is a pain in the butt. If only they saw the world as you and I do, life would be much simpler. But they don't.

And as a result, the world is filled with difficult people. There are difficult peers, co-workers, professors, bosses, family members, roommates, waiters at restaurants, baristas at Starbucks, and cashiers at Walmart. They are everywhere! So since they're all around us, instead of assuming they're all idiots, how can we learn to co-exist with these difficult people?

Every day you live life, you're attending a massive masquerade. Every one puts on masks and disguises to cover up what's really going on in their lives. How often has someone asked you how your day was going, and you replied with a casual "fine," when you knew very well that life was not fine. We all have done it. Often times when someone is acting in a negative or difficult way, it's a mask for something going on inside.

If you knew what was going on in the lives of the people you find difficult, you would be shocked. Have you ever had the experience where you're talking to a best friend, and they drop some bombshell on you of something that has been going on in their life that you had no idea about? All you knew is they seemed to be a bit more cranky or whiny or have a bad attitude lately. And while someone's situation or circumstances doesn't excuse being a jerk to others, it at least helps to know what is going on with someone else.

When you find out what's going on in someone else's life, you generally will cut them a little slack. You begin to see life through their eyes. If you were in their situation, you might be acting the same way. So when you have to deal with difficult people, remember to look past the mask and try to see life from their perspective for a moment.

If someone is negative towards you, it's generally not you they're being negative about. It may be that they're upset with their boss, their boyfriend/girlfriend or their co-worker, but it happens to be you they're taking it out on. Some people are so negative and down that they are just looking to bring others down with them or invite them to the pity party, and you just happened to receive an invitation. Don't take it personally.

Believe it or not, there are days when other people consider you difficult to be around. Shocking, I know. Sometimes when we see the negative in everyone else, maybe we're as much the problem. I remember my Mom used to tell me that in a situation when the other person is 99% wrong, and you're 1% wrong, you're still wrong. That means sometimes we need to step up to the plate and own our attitudes and actions rather than pointing the finger at someone else.

A key lesson in dealing with difficult people, and just people in general, is reminding ourselves that we can't control others. You can't control someone else's words, attitudes, or actions. You can do your part to hear them out, show them respect, and offer to help, but at the end of the day, we are only accountable for ourselves. As much as we'd like to be the puppet master to help manipulate and fix other people, life doesn't work like that. If you can't control other people, then stop trying.

chapter forty-eight
how do I get involved in community service?

Deep down we all have the desire and dream to do more than live a normal, boring, mundane existence. We desire to truly live life and to make a difference in the lives of others. We want to do more than go through the motions of life. Most of us dream of making a real impact and leaving a legacy. Maybe you feel like this. Or maybe it is the leftover pizza you ate that is talking to you. Or gas. Of course the gas may be caused by the leftover pizza. Lots of possible explanations.

Making a difference seems like one of those nice pie-in-the-sky dreams, but it doesn't always feel very realistic. We think that we are just young adults or 20-somethings, and there is nothing we could personally do that would make any type of difference. But you have an opportunity, just like anyone else, to do something and be someone that makes a difference. Here are some ideas to get you started:

think of *your* world before *the* world

Often times when we talk about making a difference, we think in terms of saving the whales, feeding the needy, curing diseases or hugging a tree. But when you begin to think about making a difference in the world, it can seem overwhelming. Personally, I'm no Mother Teresa, so making a difference like she did seems nearly impossible for someone like me. But making a difference goes beyond what we think of on a global scale. It means, before you can make a difference in *the* world, you have to first make a difference in *your* world. Where is your world? It is your community, your family, your school, your friends, your job, or any other place that you live life. You have the greatest opportunity to do something in *your* world, so start right where you're at.

start small & simple

Again, we can get so confused with doing something on such a large and grand scale that we miss out on the simplest, and sometimes most effective ways to make a difference. You don't need millions of dollars or have to be best friends with Oprah to do something significant. Sometimes, some of the best ways to make a difference are the things that are free. Think about it this way. What are some of the most memorable Christmas gifts you have ever received? Almost always, the things that are the most memorable aren't the items that cost the most, but rather had the most thought put into them. Simple things like writing a friend an encouraging note, being a shoulder for a friend to cry on during a difficult time, helping a peer study for an exam, or simply telling your parents thanks. Man, that would freak them out, wouldn't it?! It is not always the big things that matter. Sometimes it is just small and simple that makes the biggest impact.

do something

It is easy to get so consumed by thinking through how we can make the biggest difference that we end up doing nothing. On top of that, it is easy to live with the mentality of "someday" when it comes to making a difference. We think that at our age, there isn't anything of significance we can do, but nothing could be further from the truth. If you always wait until "someday" arrives before you do something to make a difference, you'll never do anything. When it comes to making a difference, doing something is almost always better than doing nothing.

connect your cause with your passion

Often times you'll find the greatest joy in service when it connects with your greatest passions. What are the causes that really get you fired up? Animal welfare? The environment? Education? Health and fitness? Human rights? Poverty? War and peace? Children? Connect with a cause that allows you to utilize your passion.

be a part of something bigger than you

I know there are certain things that as an individual, I can do to make a difference, but at the same time, I want to be part of something that is bigger than me. As I've stated before, we all have limits and a capacity to what we can do. As humans there is only so much we can do before we reach that point. But when we're part of something that is bigger than ourselves, now we're able to do so much more collectively than any one of us could do individually. Look for groups, clubs, and organizations on your campus that you can be a part of to join with others in making a difference.

In life, you can make a lot of money and be famous, have a corner office and a fancy job title, drive new cars and live in big mansions, but what does all that mean when you die? Nothing, really. But if you make a difference in the life of someone else, that is something that lives on. Whether you realize it or not, every day you are making a difference in the lives of others, both positively and negatively. Recognize and realize that you are making a difference today.

chapter forty-nine
what's my purpose in life?

This is the age old question of, "Why am I here?" Unfortunately, too often students feel like they have no purpose, meaning, or direction, and as result, they can wander aimlessly through life. In a deeper way, some students feel if they have no purpose or meaning, then there is no point to life. As a result, the depressing reality is that suicide is the third leading cause of death for teenagers.[1] This is extremely tragic because every single human life has meaning, purpose, and value. Regardless of your background or belief system, we all have purpose. Even if you don't believe you have a purpose, not believing in it doesn't make it go away. In the same way, just by believing that the Earth has no gravity doesn't mean I'm going to float into outer space.

Before you begin to answer the question of finding purpose, you have to first define what "purpose" is and isn't. Dictionary.com defines purpose as "the reason for which something exists or is done, made, used, etc." So then it seems that purpose is defined by the creator or origin of something. For example, if I create some type of contraption or device, then as the creator of the item, isn't it my responsibility to determine its purpose? Without

---

[1] http://www.teensuicide.us/articles1.html

getting into a spiritual or theological debate, finding your purpose involves asking the question, where did I come from? Personally, I believe humans were created by a loving God, and that He is involved in our daily lives. So for me, purpose and meaning stems largely from that belief.

One of the best pieces of advice I've heard regarding finding your purpose in life is to let your life speak. By this I mean, what is it in life that you are truly passionate about? What is it that you are naturally drawn to? What is it that moves you emotionally or breaks your heart? A great way to see this in action is to watch a group of children. Little kids are too young to fully comprehend all that is going on around them and probably aren't asking questions about purpose and identity quite yet. But when you're young, there are some things in life that you are just naturally drawn to more than others. There are some things you have a natural skill, talent, or ability in. It may be that you are drawn to helping others. Or you are naturally compassionate. Or you have a certain sense of justice and fairness when it comes to sharing or getting along with others. Think back to your childhood. What were the qualities and characteristics of your early years? These memories may hold the key to answering the deeper question of purpose for you.

As you search out meaning and reason for existence, let me encourage you to be patient. We live in a "microwave" culture that is looking for a quick fix or an easy answer. When it comes to determining one's purpose in life, it is not an overnight process. It takes weeks, months, and even years of searching and asking, of seeking and discovering what that looks like for you. As we've covered throughout the book, that looks different for everyone. One person's purpose may be complete confusion to another person.

In addition, purpose, like priorities, evolves over time. You may feel that your sole purpose right now is to graduate and do well in school. Or to make a difference in the lives of others. Or to refrain from beating up your little brother. All of which are noble. Because purpose evolves over time, that tells us something: we don't have to know all the answers today. It is easy to get so consumed by trying to know all the details and ins and outs of life, that we miss out on life itself. While I certainly wouldn't recommend avoiding this question altogether, I would also recommend not going to the other extreme and getting so caught up in it that life passes you by.

So what's the purpose of your life? I'm not sure that I have the perfect answer for you. I guess if I did, I should charge more for this book! But that's part of the journey of life. As I was beginning to write this book, I came across a quote that fits well in this discussion. E.L. Doctorow said, "Writing is like driving a car at night. You can see only as far as your headlights, but you can make the whole trip that way. You don't have to see where you're going, you don't have to see your destination or everything you will pass along the way. You just have to see two or three feet ahead of you." The same thing is true with life. You may not have all the answers or fully understand everything now, but if you can see a few feet in front of you, you can make the entire journey.

chapter fifty
how do I make the most of my life?

This is a great question you really have to think through and answer for yourself. Not for your friend. Not for your parents. Not for that strange kid you shared a locker with who ate glue. But for *you*, determine how you can make the most of your life. Success in life is very subjective, and what is considered to be a successful life to one person may not be as important to someone else. Consider questions like these:

- *When you die, how do you want to be remembered?*
- *What do you want people to say about you at your funeral?*
- *If you thought your life was a complete failure, what would that look like?*

If you asked 100 students these questions, you would get 100 different answers. But by answering these questions for yourself, you begin to get a better sense of how you can make the most of your life. With that in mind, here are some principles that I strive to live out in order to make the most of my life.

enjoy the journey

In the busyness and chaos that is life, it is very easy to get so bogged down in everything that you forget to enjoy the journey. Live each day to its fullest, and don't let a moment pass by. Remember those days in kindergarten with recess, nap time, and cheap milk? Those days are gone, unfortunately. Each year you get a little older (and perhaps add a few pounds), are you taking the time to smell the roses and enjoy the journey?

try something new

In life, it is very easy to live on the sidelines and always play it safe. We get into our ruts and routines and rarely do we step outside the box to take a risk and try something new. Mix it up in your life to break the routines every now and then. Order something different than the usual. Go a different route to work. Turn off the TV for a week. Take a road trip with friends. Learn a new language or skill (might I recommend nunchucks). Try something new.

you've got one life to live

At some point, all of our lives are going to come to an end. And regardless of your belief of what happens after that, you have one chance to live the life you have right now. As I write this, it is 9:17am, Tuesday, January 24, 2012. Never again will I live in this moment of time. So if I've got one life to live, then I don't want to waste a second of it. Ask yourself, "Is this the best use of this moment?"

live with no regret

There are two main types of regret. The things we do that we wish we had not done, and the things we did not do that we wish we had done. We have all done those stupid things we regret doing and will probably continue to do so throughout life, but I'm talking more about not missing out on opportunities that I will one day wish I had taken a chance at. I would rather be involved with a train wreck and know that at least I tried, than to look back someday and wonder, "What if?"

do what you love, love what you do

As we mentioned in Chapter 33, we all have to work to make a living, so personally, I would rather do something I love. Something that is more than a job or a paycheck, but something with meaning and value. Right now, I get paid to do what I love, and I can't imagine life any other way.

live on purpose

We discussed this in the last chapter, but to reiterate, nobody gets anywhere by accident. Your life isn't an accident, and you are not a mistake. Your life has purpose, meaning, and value, so you should live accordingly.

These are just a few of the things that you can do to make the most of your life. Don't wait another moment to make the most of your life. You are this age only once, so start living a life that you are proud of and that you are living on purpose.

now what?

One of my favorite questions in the world is two simple words:

Now what?

This is such a critical question, because it allows us the opportunity to do something differently based on what we've learned. How often have you heard an idea, read a book, listened to a talk, or been inspired to do something differently in your life, only to end up doing nothing? We're all guilty of it, so rather than learning just for the sake of learning, what are you going to do differently to implement what you've learned? Otherwise, what's the point? If you have no plans to apply anything you read, then there is no reason to read in the first place.

If we do things the way we've always done, we're going to continue to get the same results. That seems like common sense. It's been said that if you do things the way you've always done them and yet expect different results, it is known as insanity! It makes sense, right? So again, we come back to the question, what are you going to do differently as a result of what you've read?

As I stated in the introduction, I have no magic formula, secret pill, or special sauce that is going to change or revolutionize your life. What is going to change your life is YOU. At the risk of sounding corny or cliché, the fact is you have the ability to make your life anything that you want it to be. Regardless of your background, your family, your personality, your education, your status, or any other excuses you can come up with, you hold the power to your own destiny.

I would challenge you not only to begin to implement and apply some of these ideas into your everyday life, but also to encourage other students to do the same. If you've read something that has caused you to think or do things differently, then chances are, it would have the same effect on other students. One of the best ways that humans learn and retain information is by teaching others.

So again, not only ask yourself the question, but make a commitment that you are going to do something differently in your life. What you do from here is entirely up to you.

Now what?

Welcome to your reality check.

Your life has purpose, meaning, and value. Live accordingly.

about the author

Grant Baldwin is an engaging communicator and a leading expert at helping students prepare for life after high school. Grant is a popular motivational speaker among teens and college students and also regularly speaks at educator conferences. He has given hundreds of presentations and has spoken to over 250,000 people in 42 states through leadership conferences, college orientations, conventions, assemblies, and other student events. While Grant does love speaking and inspiring students, he loves his wife and three daughters more. They live in Springfield, Missouri.

For more info, check out www.GrantBaldwin.com.

keep in touch with grant

As you may have figured out by now, I actually really like students. It's strange I know. But beyond a book or speaking at a college or an event, I love talking with students and hearing what I can do to help them be successful in life.

If there is ever anything I can do for you, please don't hesitate to email me or give me a shout. If you've got a question, you need some advice, or you just want to let me know what you thought of *Reality Check*, I'd love to hear from you. My email address is Grant@GrantBaldwin.com.

Here are a couple of other ways to keep in touch with me:

social networks
You can track me down on various social networking sites. Here are a few links to find where I'm at:

Facebook www.facebook.com/grantbaldwinfans
Twitter www.twitter.com/grantbaldwin
YouTube www.youtube.com/grantbaldwindotcom

e-newsletter
Keep up to date through this newsletter filled with thought-provoking articles, entertaining stories, and my latest happenings and travels. Sign up at www.GrantBaldwin.com.

One last thing before you go. When you finish this book, I would encourage you to pass it on to a friend. Or better yet, just buy them their own copy! If it meant something to you, it will mean something to someone else. You never know the simple impact you can make by sharing a book!

Your Friend,

Grant

speaking engagements

Grant Baldwin is the speaker for your next orientation or college event! His blend of humorous stories and comedy with practical life skills make him a huge hit with college students on campuses across the country. Grant has delivered over 500 presentations to over 250,000 students in 42 states. He has a unique ability to capture an audience's attention with humor, yet still challenge them to think and apply action to their lives. Grant speaks at colleges, orientation sessions, welcome week events, conferences, conventions, and other events for students.

His keynote topics address issues related to personal responsiblity and taking ownership. He aims to help students realize that their transition into the real world starts now, and the person in control of creating a life worth living is YOU. He also works with student leaders and inspires them to remember how little things make a big difference in the lives of the students they work with.

Grant also provides workshops related to practical skills such as personal finance (avoiding debt, establishing credit, living on a budget, finding a job, etc.); balancing your schedule and making sense out of the chaos that life seems to be at times; and figuring out what you want to do with your life and how your passions, talents, and interests can translate into a career.

"We were extremely pleased with his performance and encourage other universities to consider Grant Baldwin for their programs. Grant's style suited new college students perfectly."
– ORIENTATION COORDINATOR, IOWA STATE UNIVERSITY

For more information or to schedule Grant to speak at your next event or orientation, please visit www.GrantBaldwin.com or contact Lisa Klug at 417.773.0989 or lisa@grantbaldwin.com.